ZEN PSYCHOLOGY

ZEN PSYCHOLOGY

"WHO IS ASKING?"

Stein Gaarder

ask–zen.com

DEDICATION

*This book is dedicated to my son Alexander
for his inspiration, wisdom and loving company.*

CONTENTS

3 THE 10 PILLARS OF ZEN
OR ZEN PSYCHOLOGY IN A NUTSHELL

4 ZEN PSYCHOLOGY

5 COMMON ZENSE: ZEN PSYCHOLOGY
APPLIED TO COMMON SENSE AND
EVERYDAY LIFE

ZEN PSYCHOLOGY

"WHO IS ASKING?"

CHAPTER 1

THE PSYCHOLOGY IN ZEN

WESTERN AND EASTERN APPROACHES TO THERAPY AND WAYS OF LIVING

Everyone in our culture suffers from the malaise of restlessness or is dissatisfied to some extent. We are never completely at ease or content in the moment of the here and now. [22] This is a symptom that something is wrong, or rather, as this book will show, that we believe erroneously that something is wrong. Zen Psychology reveals to you the delusion of believing that something is missing, that something should be improved. This delusion is the only hindrance to being in harmony with oneself as well as with other people and life's circumstances in general. However, the feeling of disharmony and the belief in a need for improvement is an extremely strong myth in our common understanding. This calls for an open mind, a willingness to look at yourself and others from a radical new point of view. That is all which is required from the reader – no more, no less. The necessary insight is provided by a happy union of Eastern philosophy and Western psychology. The ancient wisdom of the East is adopted and transformed into a modern and simple psychological framework. The result is an invitation to a radical new common understanding which would potentially permeate everyone's daily life.

The time is ripe for a radical new way of perceiving ourselves and the world around us, in short, for a new way of living. Several major and global social changes coincide and point towards a radical new understanding of who we are. There is a growing degree of conflict and unease in the personal sphere as well as in the international arena. There is an increased awareness of the inadequacy of traditional belief systems combined with the shortcomings of an endless number of improvement techniques. All are calling for a new level of consciousness which is at the same time a reunion with our original nature.

"Who is asking?" reveals how we all are great problem-makers pretending to be problem-solvers and how this pathetic but dangerous game may come to an end. [44,62,108,119,122,140,155]

This book takes you back to whom you really are which turns out to be much more than you would have dreamt of becoming. [44,54,140,141,154,156]

ZEN AND PSYCHOLOGY

Zen has never been any declared psychology or religion and definitely not had any political ambitions. If anything, Zen has been a way of living. And possibly a suggestion, a pointer for those who might happen to be interested and perhaps were about to discover it themselves. "Psychology" is our modern Western minds' way of trying to cope with our own behaviour and that of our fellow men and women. It entails first and foremost our common sense psychology, and, additionally, what we have adopted from the various psychological traditions we may have encountered. While "psychology" is a way of trying to improve ourselves, Zen is a way of understanding and direct insight. "Psychology" in a broad sense has become our Western way of living, incessantly striving for development. In a more professional sense, "psychology" is our way of healing others and ourselves. What happens when we combine Western and

Eastern ways of living? This is what this book is about. Be prepared for a lot of surprises! There will be good news and bad news. Nothing will be required from you apart from an uncompromising, open, honest mind. The time is right if you want to, but only then. Are you prepared to let go of your most precious beliefs such as your ego, self-pride, ambitions, striving for happiness and success? And likewise letting go of fear, anxiety, aggression, competitiveness, jealousy, anger and fear of failure? [14,22,121,142]

WHAT THE BOOK IS *NOT* ABOUT

It goes without saying that "psychology" is not a homogenous grouping of theories or traditions. It may even be difficult to define a common core among all the diversities. However, there are mainstreams, major traditions and certain perspectives, often grown out of well-known philosophical traditions. To pay dues to even the main psychological traditions would require a book in itself (or several). Fortunately that is not the purpose of this book. This is thus not a scholarly essay to cover the "Zen potential" or the opposite, the lack of Zen, the "non-Zense" of various psychological approaches, although that might have been a most worthwhile enterprise.

There are a lot of valuable and innovative approaches that combine Eastern philosophy, religion and "ways of living" with Western needs and thinking. [38,89,135,144] But very often they are limited to *therapy*, as in the case of adopting yoga, meditation techniques, self perception, etc. and of course they merit further investigation and development. They do represent the interest and talent of merging Eastern and Western thought about therapy, self development and well-being in general. However, as might perhaps have been expected, these approaches are usually very much on the premises of Western thinking, *at the expense of the essence and radicalism of the original Eastern philosophy*. The result is an enrichment of

Western psychology, but limited to the adoption of techniques (yoga, meditation, etc) and certain rather vague (still important, though) concepts like "mindfulness", "being in the here-and-now"and "self acceptance". It is this author's opinion that the very essence and *radicalism* of Eastern thought (notably Zen) is literally "lost in translation". In that way the strangest, the most non-Western, the greatest difference, and thus the most valuable (if true) growth for Western thought, is lost. Rather than a conservative (Western-like) "what is in it for us", as an add-on to our pre-conceived perceptions, we are going to explore "What is Zen really trying to tell?" It turns out that the message is very much more radical and provoking than one might expect. It is much more than techniques for better health or relaxation or wishful thinking about self development into higher levels of consciousness. If anything, it is rather the opposite of that. We had better be prepared, for the message is contrary not only to the main pillars of Western psychology, but foremost to some of the most self-evident and cherished "facts" and values of our common sense. (Note: for a most revealing analysis of the psychology of common sense, see J. Smedslund, 1977; A.P. Gaarder, 2019). [41,120]

WHAT ZEN IS NOT

The so-called "message from Zen" is a challenge for those prepared to think, understand and live radically differently from what we are used to. The good news is that no new theory, no belief system, no obligations, no techniques, are to be advocated or required. Those acquainted with Zen readings, will be familiar with these non-theoretical and non-directive aspects. There will be, however, plenty of suggestions and opportunities for personal re-thinking and re-living but only according to your own initiative, pace, experimenting and enjoyment. If it works, Zen is liberating and definitely does not become yet another obligation. In fact, it is the most deobligating, de-personalising and de-moralising belief system you can imagine – so be prepared!

Just as Western "psychology" is impossible to describe in both a uniform, diverse and at the same time properly representative way, the same applies to "Zen" (or Eastern philosophy, non-duality traditions in general). There are numerous traditions, many of them with impressive long heritage: 5,000 years for Advaita, 2,500 years for Buddhism, 2,000 years for Taoism, almost 1,500 years for Zen. The study of uniformity and diversity among the Zen-like traditions is a great enterprise in itself. While leaving this to the scholars, how shall we go about the issue of presenting "Zen" in a somewhat proper way? The easiest and perhaps most decent way is to focus on only the very most obvious, common fundamentals of Zen-like traditions. While acknowledging that we do not pay due respect to what may be important variations, we take the liberty of focusing on some main issues in both "Zen" and "psychology". The result is plenty of challenges! Our intention is to discover and perhaps develop some new ways of living through a psychology which is still obscure and too strange for Western thinking but has been taken care of by (the rather few) wise men and women in Eastern tradition. We may also happen to surprise ourselves and find that the old traditional Zen transforms and evolves by our very own involvement. Wow, the West is good, too!
7,23,29,38,40,56,108,128,151

WHAT THIS BOOK IS ABOUT

We shall introduce Zen Psychology through three simple steps.

1. To describe in Western terms the psychology inherent in Zen – preferably as simple, common sense rather than through academic language. It also follows that we shall take the liberty of being selective and avoid many of the esoteric traditions so unfamiliar to the Western mind such

as gurus, rigorous meditation practises or lifelong seclusion in monasteries. On the other hand, we shall do our very best to assimilate the essential Zen messages as close to their original intentions as possible. It goes without saying that the discarding of much of the cultural context of Zen or Zen Buddhism is not without pitfalls. A great deal will surely be lost. *The point is however, that so much of incredible value is nevertheless intact that it is more than most Western minds will be able to accommodate.* Whether familiar with Zen readings or not, the reader is in for a large number of challenges if he or she dares to test the suggestions in his/her own life.

In spite of the description of Eastern Zen in Western psychological terms, it will become evident how radical (and therefore different and useful) Zen is. It will emerge how surprising, how personal, how mind-blowing, how simple yet challenging, Zen is for everyone sufficiently curious to investigate something completely new and contrary to previous beliefs.

2. Show the difference between Zen and common sense. Provide exercises and guidance for the practising in everyday life.

3. Develop traditional Zen through interaction with Western psychology into "Zen Psychology".

The Eastern traditions may not be the last and final saying in understanding human consciousness and behaviour. Without really disputing the essential paradoxes of Zen, like no-theory (concepts), no-language (only pointers), no-development, it turns out to be possible to transcend these show-stoppers. How? You are entitled to ask. By using Zen on Zen. Zen emphasises the validity and basics of everyday life and consciousness. In that respect we are all experts. Common sense (including daily experiences and problems) provides us with ample evidence and examples of what is real and what is illusionary, what makes sense and what is non-Zense. When this is uncovered here and recognised by yourself in your everyday life, you have all you need for going – or being – your own natural way, whatever that may be. This may sound a little more serious and ambitious than intended. Liberation is, if anything, fun and playful. It is not a serious matter. According to Zen (disregarding the rigorous, scholastic traditions). [137,138,139]

PSYCHOLOGY: THE SCIENCE OF MIND AND BEHAVIOUR

Here is one commonly used definition of psychology:

"Psychology is the teaching of mental and physical behaviour"

("Philosophy of Psychology", Bermudez, (Ed.), 2006). [16]

One has to start somewhere. Then, this definition of "Psychology" may serve as a good start as any. However, even at this very outset, there is at least one preconception in psychology which is taken for granted (either by society/ culture, common sense or scientific/philosophical traditions), and which is fundamentally wrong, a misunderstanding – if Zen is right. The implication is that the whole basis, the very fundament of "Psychology" in most of its variants is a blind alley, a wrong direction, a deception, a sometimes even futile, self-contradicting enterprise. [22,77,97,144]

It might perhaps be possible to describe this fundamental difference as just one single issue – and we shall also have a simple shot at that. However, it may be even more instructive to look at some of the main implications. Every one of these implications may in fact serve as an illustration, a pointer, of the basic fallacy (if Zen is right). These main implications or controversies with traditional Psychology, and even with Common sense, shall therefore be the topics of this chapter.

The basic concept of "psychology" has one or two very important implications.

a) "The Mind" as such is an independent (at least to some degree) phenomenon (or activity, process, function, object), as distinct from the Environment (and physical body) of the human organism. In other words, the Mind is seen as an Object, wholly or partly **apart** (separate, distinct) from the Environment/surroundings. This is of course the core of the philosophical tradition of "dualism". [16,45,68,86]

b) In addition, the concept of "Psychology" implies that this phenomenon may be observed, studied, understood and described. Thereupon, it may also be altered, improved, developed or repaired (as in therapy). This item b) is perhaps somewhat secondary or implicit in item a), since the acceptance of something as an independent "object" also presupposes some kinds of attributes which may be described and investigated. [7,16,41,122]

ZEN VERSUS PSYCHOLOGY: THE NON-ZENSE OF PSYCHOLOGY AND COMMON SENSE

We shall of course avoid arguing against an old-fashioned version of "psychology" with its complete dichotomy between body and mind, or between mind and matter. The dualism weakens in accordance with how much the psychological traditions have developed into interactive perspectives, social relationships, interconnectedness, interdependence, social contexts or psycho-somatic processes. However, from the Zen point of view, they are still fundamentally dualistic in the sense of differentiating between the observer and the observed. [15,77,8 9,90,92,95,97,100,118,122]

It should be accepted that Psychology as such has neither the honour nor the blame for being the first to treat the psyche (mind) as a separate phenomenon. This inclination is already firmly embedded in Common sense and thus runs back to ancient times. The dualism and substantiality of the mind are apparently confirmed by each individuals relatively consistent behaviour (= "personality"), the difference between people (= "different personalities"), the difference between children and adults (= "growth"), the difference between groups of people (= "culture"). [51,52]

But foremost of all the apparent manifestations of the mind is the subjective experiences of an inner life, with thoughts, emotions and the inner dialogue with oneself. The inner voice – for most people constituting a continuous stream of considerations, wishes and concern – is for everyone the very manifestation or proof of an "I", an Ego, of Being, of existing. As if this were not sufficient, the Ego-feeling intensifies whenever there is a conflict or tension related to the Environment: doubt, fear, aggression, desire. We then experience Will, Choice (Free will), and we believe even more strongly in ourselves as Acting persons (when we feel in control) but also as overly vulnerable Victims (when the Environment is controlling us). [90,95,122]

The psychology inherent in common sense reveals a common and effective system for how we characterise other people, the environment and ourselves. Examples of such characteristics are: to Know, Wish, Want, Do, Think, Feel, etc. [41,120,122] The dualistic concepts dividing Person/Environment are included in the common sense vocabulary. This common system constitutes our shared "Psychology", including both values and experience accumulated over time. But even this most basic common sense is not necessarily correct. According to Zen, it is far off track. Or more precisely, our common sense manifests a natural but not very advanced stage in the development of consciousness.

Now the cat is out of the bag…. So far we have just presented a lot of preposterous postulations and we shall use the rest of the reader's patience – if there still is some curiosity left – to reveal which cat we are talking about. The intention so far has been to give an early warning about the Zen message as being a very radical alternative to Psychology, even so radical that it counters common sense and some of our most accepted and cherished "truths". [94,123,139,140,143]

WHAT IS ZEN, THEN?
(THE CAT IS OUT OF THE BAG)

The nature of the Zen alternatives is to show the illusion of the old truths, rather than promote new theories or concepts. Moreover, the Zen suggestions point back to your own experiences and insight, a kind of re-discovering of your original mind or "psychology" (!) in the sense of immediate and direct contact with your own nature and spontaneous interaction with an environment which is not outside and apart from yourself but is really a part of yourself, or is really you (or even You).

If Zen has no theory of its own, what can it possibly have to offer as a replacement when it has done away with a substantial part of modern psychology as well as our most cherished (although in reality frustrating, futile and disappointing) jewels of common sense? What do we get in return, except for a lot of scepticism and lost human treasures (such as free will, being rational and having control, believing in morality, mastery of nature and combatting evil?) What is the use of tearing down (or trying to tear down) what has taken us hundreds (or even thousands) of years to achieve?

The answer to this crucial question is simpler than one might expect: we regain our spontaneous reality. A re-discovery or un-covering of our original Nature, which never really left us and which is un-avoidable even in our most virtual and self-imposed confusions. Nor did we, or can we, really deviate from the natural flow of events. But as long as we think we can, and keep trying, and keep lying to ourselves, and keep believing in the strong ego in an alien world, we shall continue to suffer these self-inflicted conflicts, fear, frustrations, despair, sorrow or just dissatisfaction and the feeling that there is something missing. We do not "get" anything from Zen, but we regain our sanity and wholeness, and are again free to enjoy whatever happens – thereafter. Zen is not the goal or end result, Zen is the beginning. [55,84,87,102,104,110,143]

THE FUNDAMENTALS OF PSYCHOLOGY – AS OPPOSED TO ZEN

It goes without saying that Psychology as well as Zen are represented by so many and such different traditions and techniques that no single categorisation will pay due respect to all the variations. Nevertheless, there are a limited number of main philosophical traditions which cover quite a lot of the basis for contemporary psychological theories and practices. (For simplification, we disregard the blending of theories and almost limitless diversity of practices). One useful framework is offered in "Philosophy of Psychology". (Bermudez, (Ed.), 2006). [16]

Traditional philosophy of mind focuses on the mind/body problem. How are individual mental states related to physical states and behaviour? The different "solutions" offered may be said to reflect the basis of several mainstreams of contemporary psychological theories and practice. [12,64,89,121]

Four different perspectives are introduced to cover the spectrum of philosophical/psychological viewpoints. The perspectives represent four levels ranging from the most physical level of the neuro-computational theories, then the representational ones, the functional theories and finally those postulating an autonomous mind. All the perspectives are of course aware of the other possible ways of describing human behaviour

and, also accordingly offer their explanations for events that
apparently appear on other levels. For instance, even the neuro-
computational models must also account for "higher-level"
events such as learning, problem solving, emotions, intentions,
conflicts, etc. The picture of the neuro-computational mind is
inspired by the analogy between the brain and computer, the
brain's neural networks and the artificial (?!) digital networks.
This level postulates a co-evolution where our understanding of
commonsense psychology co-evolves with our understanding
of the neural basis of cognition. [17] The next level is the picture
of the representational mind. Here there are still analogies
to computers but now only to "operations" (software and
human ware): operations of language, thinking and behaviour.
The third level of explanations is represented by the picture
of the functional mind. Here commonsense psychological
explanations are granted causal validity, no more or no less
mystical than causal explanations from science and the physical
world. There is no fundamental distinction between the personal
and the sub-personal levels of explanation, according to the
functional point of view. The fourth level is the autonomous
mind, where there is postulated a discontinuity between
commonsense explanations and the sub personal levels. The
mind is autonomous, independent and interacts only indirectly
with the lower levels of explanations and materialistic causality.
This personal level may be understood by its own premises and
cannot be reduced to, nor additionally explained by physical
events at the lower levels. [155,160]

In our context, the most significant feature of these four
perspectives is that they all take for granted a kind of
dichotomy between mind/body or mind/world. Although they
differ fundamentally in describing the *interaction*, they are
all variants of the basic split between the organism and the
environment, thereby implying a *dualism*, one way or another.

Zen on the other hand, postulates that the very dualism as
such must be transcended if we are to understand the human

way of life. [61,62,88,89] Apparently, this is an even more mentalist approach than the fourth level of the autonomous mind. Right or wrong, the non-dualistic strategy leads to a challenging and surprising questioning of many "truths" in psychology as well as in common sense.

CHAPTER 2

ZEN IN PSYCHOLOGY

Several trends in modern psychology advocate interactive perspectives: "positive psychology", "interdependence", social contexts. Despite being developed in genuine Western traditions, their resemblance to Zen, Buddhist or Eastern psychology is striking. Secondly, there are a growing number of explicit and promising attempts to adopt Eastern philosophy into Western concepts and practices, especially within clinical cognitive psychology. Examples such as "mindfulness" and "acceptance meditation" are sometimes translated into contemporary cognitive and behavioural therapy. [15,16,22,38,135,145]

However, something is "lost in translation". What is missing, before we may speak of any "Zen psychology", is a radical and complete framework expressing the essence of Zen: Zen from a psychological point of view. This framework should not be limited to therapy and relaxation techniques, but primarily address everyday psychology and common sense.

ZEN THERAPY

The adoption of Zen into Western Psychology seems mainly to have been motivated by "what can we get out of it" from a *therapeutic* point of view. There is nothing wrong with that strategy, except that it may miss the radical relevance of

Zen for everybody, not only for recognised displaced people. We shall have a look at one brilliant adaptation of Zen into Western therapy. For us, this will also serve as an introduction of the basic flavour of Zen as distinct from traditional Western psychology.

There are of course a whole spectrum of mental and physical methods, theories and healing techniques, ranging from the most scientific and academically accepted approaches of medicine, psychiatry and psychology to the more esoteric ones like "alternative" medical or spiritual exercises. I shall not even attempt to categorize these, much less provide an overview of the thousands of theories and techniques flourishing and thriving on modern societies' anxiety and stress. No doubt there are myriads of interesting and valuable approaches which may work for some time or perhaps work as long as you believe in them. However, having been touched (or contaminated) with Zen, you are apt to lose quite a lot of belief in *any* system and consequently also a reduced need for seeking the ultimate technique or answer to your life problems.

I am thus taking the liberty of being very selective and I am chosing but a few approaches for the case of demonstrating the radicalism of Zen. One very illustrating approach is the one of David Brazier (1995) showing how Zen and Psychology may be combined. [22]

Most spiritual ways indicate the continuity or at least the relatedness between the "normal" healthy state of mind and "abnormal" unhealthy states, usually supplemented with a prescription (or several!) for transcendence (or healing). This goes also for psychological traditions and likewise for Zen. [90,91,144,147]

ZEN AS A WAY OF LIVING

In the book "Zen Therapy" (1995) Brazier describes the origin of Zen as a philosophy, a form of Buddhism and a form of psychology. [22] But most of all Zen is "a way of living" or a way of being completely alive. "Buddhism is the way of spiritual liberation which finds it origins in the experience of enlightenment". He goes on to trace its origin to India 25 centuries ago (!). "Zen is rooted in experience, rather than ideas." It is, in the famous words of Bodhidharma:

A special transmission outside the teachings,
Not relying upon the written word,
Directly pointing to the heart,
Seeing its nature and becoming Buddha.

The Eastern philosophies and religions may be rather unfamiliar to most Western people and provoke unnecessary objections or obscurity. I believe that the essence of Zen does not necessarily require much knowledge, even less adherence to ancient Eastern culture. This is also the very reason that we may allow ourselves the liberty to look at Zen from a more familiar Western "psychological" viewpoint. However, we shall adopt several quotes from Brazier to provide us with a minimum level of knowledge of the Buddhist concepts.

THE NORMAL, RESTLESS MIND
IS THE CHALLENGE

Brazier: "To grow pearls there has to be some grit in the oyster. Each of us has our gritty question. All too often, however, we devote our lives to ignoring rather than working on it. According to Zen, it is this ignoring (avidya) which keeps us in the realm of suffering (samsara), but it is the grit (dukkha) which gives us the opportunity to liberate ourselves." [22] "We are born weeping and we die protesting. In between we hate getting older, getting sick, becoming tied up with circumstances we dislike, and being separated from the things we do like. There is never a time when we are totally at ease. The body never feels completely comfortable from one minute to the next. Even more so the mind. Not only that, but these bad states can have terrible consequences in the form of wars, persecutions, strife, competition, oppression and cruelty". Here Brazier with a few words indicates the common nature of inner well-being and outer harmony as well as its opposite, inner restlessness (dis-ease!) and outer conflict. Also, we sense the continuum or degree of unrest from the "normal" (= usual) nervousness to the more extreme dissatisfaction and disharmony. This is one way of seeing that Zen is a way of living. Another central point here is the description of the so-called normal state as relatively unhealthy, dissatisfactory, neurotic. *This normal, ordinary, restless mind is the challenge to Zen.* More neurotic or more violent behaviour is essentially just an extreme version of the common dis-ease bothering all mankind. Zen development (or rather, insight) is thus primarily a way for everyone, only secondarily a therapy for those who need it most as such. Brazier however, shows how it may work as therapy. In fact, from his point of view Zen is essentially therapy. He makes a comparison with Western schools of therapy which help us get "the dragon back to the cave". We will thus "be returned to what Freud called "ordinary unhappiness" and heave a sigh of relief temporarily as our repressions are working smoothly once again. Zen, by contrast, offers dragon-riding lessons, for the few who are sufficiently intrepid".

From his long experience as a practitioner Brazier confirmed that his clients' lives and troubles did not differ from his own: pain and confusion, frustrations and fears. Suffering arising from the desire for security, recognition and comfort, escape from disease, pain and loss. In short, his clients as well as he longed for a world which does not exist: an ego-centred universe. "We all dream of unreal worlds where we will never be embarrassed nor thwarted. We suffer great frustration in consequence. As soon as we stop doing so, we are free".

To stop doing so is of course easier said than done. [26,27,35,61,62,78,137,149] This is what Zen is about. And its radical approach may at first seem very suspect and contrary to self-evident truths (or assumptions) in traditional psychology as well as in common sense.

"According to Buddhism then, there are not many people who are really psychologically healthy. Most of those who do manage to live relatively stable lives do so more because of fortunate circumstances than real stability." [22] "On the other hand, Zen is extremely generous in attributing an unspoiled, perfect nature to everyone anywhere anytime, a true nature which is unavoidable and only seemingly clouded (hidden from awareness) by the turmoil of the mind". There will be lots of apparent paradoxes like this one later.....But without challenges there would not be anything really new?

CONTROLLING THE SELF
– A CURSE OR A BLESSING?

According to Buddhist psychology, neurosis derives from self-seeking. (NB! Please notice how this statement is contrary to most therapeutic or self improvement techniques). [5,65,66,71,77,85,97,103,110,154,157]

"If we are all part of one another, then the actualization of our true nature will be something which intrinsically creates harmony. If we are all separate individuals, then the actualization of each self is liable to bring us into conflict with one another." "Buddhist psychology thus challenges the individualistic foundation of conventional psychology." "... Western psychology generally leans toward the idea of a self, soul or psyche which exists as an entity in its own right and which can make demands and claims. This is all in accord with long-standing Western traditions where, especially in America, a culture has been created around the idea of individual rights and needs. Buddhist psychology, however, recognizes no such entity". (Brazier, 1995) [22]

The Western and the Zen perspectives have two different views on ethics deriving from the different views of what a person is. "From the Western perspective ethics and morality are generally conceived as limiting factors curbing the excesses of the individual. Frustration follows; we hate to live by "shoulds" and "ought to's". "The growth in popularity of humanistic and positive psychology probably owes something to the desire to rebel against restrictive morality. In Zen, ethics are not seen as a restriction, but as a liberation. They are the way to realize our core nature and consequently are the path of truth and happiness. Moral codes are simply an approximate description of the life of a fully-realized being."

"Finally, in the very brief review of east-west parallels, we must mention the recent development of transpersonal psychology. Here the influence of the East is direct and acknowledged. The transpersonal approach is, in some ways, a reaction to humanism. Humanism, linked to the idea of "self-actualization", proved to be both individually liberating and culturally fragmenting. It was, in a word, narcissistic. 'We pay a high price for our illusion of autonomy – in the form of loneliness, unsatisfying relations with mates and families, longing for a sense of community...' "Ecological and transpersonal visions provide a bridge between Western and Zen psychologies. In Zen, one might say, the self has always been green. Zen culture is close to nature. Go for a walk. Sit by a waterfall. Hug a tree. Feel the rain on your skin. Direct perception of nature brings us back to our original sanity."

"The way of Zen is thus supremely practical. [22] Although we all tie ourselves up in knots with our ideas and feelings, the way through generally begins with acting purposefully now. Know your purpose at this moment and there is no difficulty knowing what to do. Paradoxically, perhaps, being able to act this way means letting go of trying to control tomorrow, or yesterday. Simply do the right thing now".

"The basic exercise of Zen is to sit in meditation and quieten the mind. This is called zazen ('za' = sitting). A Zen therapist needs to use this practice regularly and, in suitable cases, it can be taught to clients. Zazen is a direct antidote to stress, and a powerful aid in breaking habits. Zazen is like allowing a glass of muddy water to clear. The water will clear by itself if we stop shaking it for a while. Inner calm requires stillness. In particular, Zen practitioners have discovered, the best way to control the mind is to control the body. When the body is perfectly still, the mind quietens down".

There is a parallel in Buddhist theories and the psychoanalytical one: our lives are full of images of objects which are not really present and these influence us in most of our activities. Mental states all hang upon the perception of objects, which may or may not be present. The objects we perceive therefore are, unless we are completely enlightened, all shaped and coloured by a personal agenda or intention. They are **conditioned**. This personal agenda constitutes our attachment to self. In Buddhist psychology, there is a particular object which distorts all other perceptions. This object is **me**. It may seem strange, at first, to think of ourselves as an object. Surely our self is the subject who perceives, rather than the object perceived. According to Buddhist psychology, the self as perceiver is not something we can ever directly perceive. *Such a self does not exist. Nonetheless, we do hold many images of ourselves in mind. These images are imaginary objects.* They are not really present, but are images which we use to make sense (or nonsense) of our experience. In Buddhist psychology then, self is an unreal object which tends to dominate our perception and distort our relation to the world. [9,10,30,31,70,97,130,131,132,149,150,155]

ME AND NOT-ME, THE PRIMAL MISTAKE
OF SPLITTING THE UNIVERSE

"William James, the great nineteenth-century psychologist, when writing about how our minds choose some things and reject others, and how such choices can be much the same for many people, goes on to say: 'There is, however, one extraordinary case in which no two men are known to choose alike. One great splitting of the universe into two halves is made by each of us; and for each of us almost all of the interest attaches to one of the halves; but we all draw the line of division between them in a different place. When I say that we all call the two halves by the same names, and that those names are "me" and "not-me" respectively, it will at once be seen what I mean'. (James, 1890, p.289, in Brazier, 1995). [22]

Zen and all Buddhism, is an attempt to overcome the 'great splitting of the universe' to reveal its delusionary nature and to restore us to the original cosmic unity, not just as a piece of academic knowledge, but as an experienced reality." [96,142]

"All psychotherapy is concerned with understanding what is going on when people are 'not themselves'. This much used colloquialism is recognizable as meaningful to nearly all of us even though logic tells us it does not make sense. How can one not be oneself? " [22]

"In conventional psychological terminology, conditions such as depression, anxiety and obsession are all referred to as 'disorders'. It does not however, take a lot of thought to realize that this is an abuse of the English language. The thoughts and behaviour of a person suffering from any of these distressing conditions are far more orderly than those of people who are living happy, varied, socially engaged lives. The depressed person and the anxious person both tend to think the same thing over and over again while the obsessional person does the same thing over and over. These are not states in which there is a deficiency of order. They are states in which there is a superfluity of it, a hyper-order rather than a disorder. What the depressed, anxious or obsessional person needs is to become more disordered rather than less." [22]

DEVELOPING OR WEAKENING THE SELF?

Here is a major difference between East and West:

"That the weakening of the self is taken to be a desirable end is generally seen as one of the most significant differences between Buddhist and Western psychology. The latter is generally concerned with feeding the ego. Numerous attempts have been made to reconcile this divide between the theories which is considerably confused by the fact that usage of the terms 'self' and 'ego' is far from consistent. "Strengthening the ego" can mean gaining in courage and it can also mean being more selfish. It can mean overcoming one's undesirable habits and it can mean 'thinking about myself for a change'. The first of each of these pairs is part of giving up self, while the second is part of giving in to it. Most ordinary people, when they say some such thing as 'That person is all ego', are using the term in the Buddhist rather than the Western sense." [22] If we were about to choose just one significant Zen principle, it would certainly be the one about the Ego.

SO WHAT?

After these introductory descriptions of the main differences between Zen (or Buddhist psychology in general) and Western psychology, we shall focus primarily on what Zen really means psychologically. Taking the liberty of putting much of the mysticism aside, likewise the honourable traditions of philosophy and Eastern religion, disciplines and rituals – we then ask "what does it really mean to us?" What's in it for me? What does it mean that I am already there? What are the implications, the consequences? And why is it said to turn common sense upside down? And my everyday life?

We shall now try to identify the actual *psychological principles of Zen*, independent of therapy as such. It is as a general way of living – of understanding oneself and others – that Zen may have the most profound impact. The greatest impact will probably not be on psychology itself, but on common sense. This book will not be the final word on this matter, to say the least. At best it may trigger others to investigate further, to make Zen more sensible for Western minds and to find surprises in the combination (and controversy) of Zen, psychology and common sense.

CHAPTER 3

THE 10 PILLARS OF ZEN

OR

ZEN PSYCHOLOGY IN A NUTSHELL

INTRODUCTION

What do we mean by "Zen Psychology"? The most important part of this is the psychology inherent in Zen, in appreciation of the wisdom and principles of the ancient traditions and their many translations into Western culture. Of course, much is lost in translation (and we shall do our best not to take this lightly). The point is rather that so much is nevertheless taken care of, provided we are open to radical ideas about ourselves. Secondly, not everything from old Eastern traditions is necessarily beneficial in our cultural setting such as gurus, lifelong seclusion, rigorous discipline, etc. Thirdly, our culture may also have a say, and who knows – some surprises may pop up. If anything, we know that free questioning and personal understanding is completely in accordance with the spirit of Zen rather than loyal reverence for the old masters. This is our daring justification for adopting and adapting Zen into Zen Psychology.

THERE IS NO SECRET

If there in ancient times was any secret in Zen, it was simply the (profound) message that there is no secret. Reality is there for everyone to see. No knowledge, education, development, physical or mental exercises, improvement nor theories of any kind are required. Such techniques do not help. In fact, they are almost always a hindrance because they are misleading and postpone the actual realisation of truth. Even worse, the search for improvement or development is, in principle, the very reason for not seeing things as they are. What can we do then, you and I, when there is nothing to do? When working on yourself does not work? That's when the journey really starts. That's when we start to grow up and stop believing in Santa Claus (or any other belief system). That's when this book starts. 2,6,39,67,75,79,80,146

If there is no secret, what is there, then? For a start there is the false belief that there *is* a secret, that there is something else, which is unknown, that you need to do before you can be happy (or whatever you are missing). Something is wrong. What am I doing wrong? If there is one thing I am sure of, it is that I am not happy, or not happy enough. Or, at least, I could have been happier. "I grieve, therefore I am not" (what I should be). Either way I need to pull myself together or I need help. Or both – which is the psychology or almost the religion of today.

WHO IS ASKING?

Whether I turn outwards for help or apparently inwards for improvement, I actually turn away from myself, *away from the one who is asking*. We are seeking improvement, apparently with good intentions. But what we are doing is really an escape, away from the questioner, away from the subject. The very question itself, the urge, the need, the motivation, the craving, the helplessness, is the escape itself and thus the problem itself.

No wonder whatever we find in that direction does not work. The bad news is that the question (or the one who asks and seeks) is the problem. The good news is that the question is also the answer, the solution or rather dissolution of the problem. In the moment the questioner is becoming aware of herself or himself, the question dissolves and with it the need for finding some "other" solution or answer. The question is a constructed, a construed problem.

We make it up and then pretend that we did not make it ourselves in the first place. Often we forget about the whole thing, thereby making it unconscious and thus even less available. WHY? Why on earth do we play this peculiar trick on ourselves? That's a good question and deserves a lot of consideration, but we must save some goodies for later.

To understand and acknowledge ourselves as the problem-makers is a major challenge. It is, in fact, THE challenge. This calls for reflection, meditation, introspection, experimenting and careful observing. A great deal. Fortunately, every one of us has plenty of problems to consider and observe. You may start with any one of your personal hindrances, i.e. situations you are uncomfortable with, avoiding or are anxious about, people you dislike, times when you are emotionally upset, when you are in disagreement with yourself, dwelling on the past, fearing the future, blaming yourself, blaming others. For a start... It is important to remember that the negative emotions themselves are not bad, they are justified and should not be repressed or condemned. However, they are *symptoms* of things being misunderstood, of problems being made – here and now, in the very moment you are having the emotions. The easing of the emotions is likewise a sure sign that you are on the right track of dissolving the construed conflict. Be aware whenever this happens. It is gold and can be used deliberately to encourage you to face other challenges, too.

WHY WORKING ON YOURSELF DOES NOT WORK

Mainstream self-help techniques, whether they are traditional or "alternative", all turn up with "recipes" to solve or heal the supposed problem of unhappiness or people not being in accord with themselves or with their fellow beings. What if "the problem" is false? What if the very questions we ask again and again, are just symptoms of an underlying major (primal) Misunderstanding? If so, we are just fooling ourselves while looking for solutions in all the wrong directions, no matter whether they are called behavioural, bodily or mental exercises. When one technique does not work, there are hundreds of others you should try. "Have you not met my guru yet?" "Have you not heard about 'The Secret'"? "You should try my therapist". The recommendations and well-meaning help are endless. It is time to stop fooling yourself (and others). It is time to grow up. [77,102]

THE PRIMAL MISTAKE

Thousands of years ago Zen (and similar traditions and precursors like Taoism) recognised that the primal Mistake (or original Sin) is the belief in "Ego", the vision of ourselves as an independent agent in an external world. This egocentricity is the root of alienation, disharmony and the neverending struggle to once again become reconciled with ourselves as well as with the world around us. We have put ourselves at the centre of the universe (as on a pedestal), but at the expense of being left out, being at the outside, being "the others", being alien. *We* are the aliens! The result is fear and distrust or hostility. The more the Ego strives, the more is the divide accentuated, uncomfortable and dangerous. No wonder that all the promising techniques for working on yourself do not work. When nothing can be done, what can we do, then?! That's the question. This is where the psychology of Zen begins. [57,58,59,60,134,138]

THE QUESTION IS THE ANSWER

When there is no answer to a question, perhaps the question itself is wrong or false? What if we ourselves created the problem in the first place? Or even worse, what if we are re-creating the problem at the very same moment we are asking how to solve it? If we ourselves created the problem from the very outset, then any seeking, any attempt at solving it, any questioning is actually an escape, a pretence. It is a guaranteed method of never finding a solution. This of course suits the same motivation which inspired the creation of the problem in the first place. *Zen psychology reveals how we all are great problem-makers pretending to be problem-solvers and how this pathetic but dangerous game may come to an end*. It is time to grow up and let go of our lollipops!

Mainstream professional help, self-help or "alternative" trends – they all try to heal problems that are often created (or perpetuated) by the individuals themselves. Why doesn't working on oneself work? Because we are the ones who create the problem in the first place, then earnestly try to solve it (by help or self-help) and look everywhere else apart from back to the original troublemaker. Myriads of purported success stories are part of the game. [97]

"Who is asking?" brings you back to the root of the problem, the basic Misunderstanding that led you astray. This is a return to sanity and your real self. This is the end of the need for control, the end of longing for peace of mind, or the end of just missing "something". But be prepared: the new self-insight may reveal something other than what you expected.

Why don't all the good intentions work? Wishful thinking is only part of the problem. Worse is the search in the wrong directions, that is anywhere else rather than towards the seeker herself or himself. The most ardent and conscientious approaches are all dead ends because they are chasing a

ghost; the belief in an Ego, the independent agent supposed to be responsible, intelligent, free and in control of our life. It does not matter whether my focus is on "internal" (mental) or "external" (behavioural) problems, in both cases attention is directed towards something *other* than the one who seeks and thus creating the very alienation (duality, otherness) that one pretends to eliminate or reduce (so-called improvement or development). I would be better off chasing my own shadow.
27,28,61,77

ZEN PSYCHOLOGY IN A NUTSHELL

An entirely new development for Western psychology will be revealed.

It combines the best from east and west – avoiding Eastern as well as Western myths – and lets us re-discover the truths of common sense and our natural sanity. In this commonsense view of everyday life, the laymen are encouraged to be experts as well as the professionals.

Zen is here developed into a psychological framework, but one that is grounded in common sense. The message is better conveyed in everyday language than in academic terms. In fact, from a Zen perspective, understanding is best enhanced through just pointing directly to our shared everyday or common life experiences.

The following paragraphs present the essence of Zen – *from a psychological point of view*. It is an attempt to investigate the fundamental *working* principles, across different Eastern traditions and across different Western interpretations. The challenge is of course, not to misunderstand the original wisdom or twist it into old Western concepts. On the other hand, provided we have an understanding of what it is all about, we will allow ourselves the freedom to experiment with new viewpoints. The following 10 core concepts of Zen are offered as a complete system of Zen Psychology, no more, no less. They may well be seen as a guidance for 10 ways of living, but they are all pointing at one and the same insight. Later on, we shall look at more familiar everyday experiences (or life problems we all have in common) and see how they are rooted in and solved by these 10 pillars of Zen.

There is one peculiar attribute common to most of the principles: they are negations, suggesting that we stop fooling ourselves rather than urging us to correct and improve. The principles are pointers for us to trust spontaneity and the natural flow of events. The negative principles signify behaviour we can "do" something about, or more precisely: letting go, stopping doing. The positive principles signify behaviour we neither can nor need to do anything about (Spontaneity, Acceptance, Liberation). They are already given and perfect in every individual's nature. No development or change is necessary (or possible). They appear whenever they are not over-shadowed by the negative behaviour principles.

The arrows drawn in the figure between the principles indicate both a pattern and a progression. The pattern is simply the relationship between principles being close to each other. The progression signifies our consciousness development towards liberation. There will be much more about this in later chapters. First we shall have a look at each one of the principles or guidance for living. Each one of them is a challenge and an invitation to growth but only if we allow them to be so.

ZEN PSYCHOLOGY IN A NUTSHELL

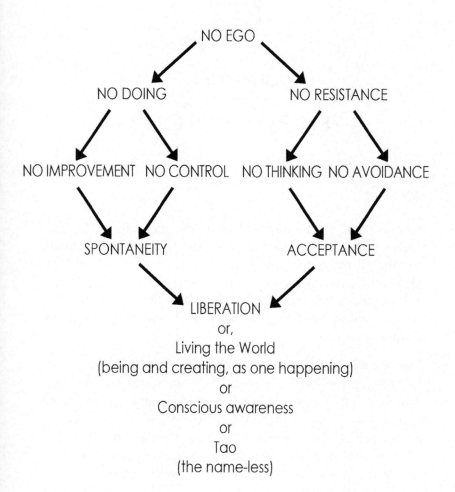

NO EGO

NO DOING → NO RESISTANCE

NO IMPROVEMENT NO CONTROL NO THINKING NO AVOIDANCE

SPONTANEITY ACCEPTANCE

LIBERATION
or,
Living the World
(being and creating, as one happening)
or
Conscious awareness
or
Tao
(the name-less)

CHAPTER 4

ZEN PSYCHOLOGY

NO EGO

If we should select one and only one item from the Zen
teachings, it must be the one about the Ego or Egoless mind.
Perhaps all the other aspects may even be derived from this
one and they only serve to explain its meaning or implications.
Unfortunately, this central principle is also the most difficult to
transmit, not because it is complex, but because it is so contrary
to common sense.

What do we associate with the concept of "Ego"? Apart from
the negative connotation of "egoistic", too much ego, the term
signifies what is most precious, most close and most personal
for every one of us. It is the I, the me, myself, me as a person,
me as distinct from the rest of the world. From "my" point of
view, we are all at the very centre of the universe, both as a
part of it and as observing it. We are aware of ourselves in
two different modes, as a subject (in direct and spontaneous
interaction with the "environment") and as a object (when
looking at ourselves from the outside, observing ourselves – as
when seeing a picture or video of ourselves, or hearing about
ourselves from others, or thinking about ourselves).

With reflective capacity we are able to see (think, imagine) ourselves as objects, from the apparent outside. We then see a particular mind/body organism with certain characteristics, a certain personal history, preferences and behaviours.

Even more personal than my mind/body organism, is my consciousness. This is what I primarily mean by my Ego, myself, my self. My conscious thinking, feelings, desires, perceptions and actions. Especially my thinking, the constant chatting with myself, my judgement of what is being observed, my consideration of alternative actions and my choices, feedback and new choices. Particularly my intentions and their fulfilment or obstructions. My consciousness is looking after me, taking care of me, making adjustments. So far, so good. But not according to Zen. We have already made a mistake, in fact The Big Mistake. [8,28,93,98,112,119,136,141,145,153]

What can possibly be wrong in the description (concept, image) of ourselves (the Ego, the mind/body organism) in interaction with the environment? As objects, the description is obviously correct (objects = we see ourselves apparently from the outside, imagine ourselves, look through the eyes of others). As subjects, it is not correct at all, and it is as subjects we are actually functioning, i.e. living, feeling, thinking, acting. We may however, imagine (believe, think, pretend) that we are functioning as objects (separate organisms), thereby creating confusion, disparity or incongruence between our self image and ourselves, between how we are and how we think we are. What we are thinking about ourselves is then different from what we are feeling about ourselves. And we have sided with the thinking. This is the general neurosis for everyone. A general discomfort, dissatisfaction, urge to improve oneself, urge to criticize others, perception of conflict. The greater disparity, the greater discomfort and confusion. The more congruence, the more feeling of inner harmony and less experience of outer conflicts. (These variations are of course accentuated by the interaction with external circumstances, like more or less provoking/supporting behaviour of our fellow beings).

There is a trap here, alluring us into the thinking mode. When talking about this, we are necessarily in the thinking mode (concepts, language, images). Then the object-description (of a separate, individual organism interacting with the environment) seems inevitably correct. Fortunately we have not lost our spontaneous, subjective consciousness. Fortunately we cannot lose it at all. It is the way we function and live regardless of how confused and screwed up we might have become. When seen from within (ourselves as subjects), we thus have direct access to this subjective way of living (whether the activity of the moment is thinking, feeling or acting). I shall soon appeal to your own experiences, your observations, providing examples of this direct subjectivity, which is the most direct, simple, non-mystical thing in the world. However, this direct subjectivity is antipathetic to words, being so concrete that its mere conceptualisation, even naming, makes it vanish into thin air. We are thus totally dependant on our (me and everyone) own subjective experience, ability and willingness to look within introspectively, to see what is happening – before you start theorizing about it.

This kind of personal understanding and subjective experience is, by the way, what is required for any Zen understanding to have any effect. Theoretical understanding may also be quite useful and sometimes act as pointers sooner or later, but it is never the real thing. [21,124,156]

Exercise

The subjective experience is what is called "on first (1.) evidence" by Douglas D. Harding, referring to you as the first person, the first witness. [55,56,58] When you are looking at some external object, say the tree outside your window – what do you see? You see just the tree itself, you do not see yourself as the perceiver, just the tree. But the tree is *your* experience, your consciousness, in that moment. In that sense, the tree is you. Or you are the tree. Wow, that is something?! Please take a moment to observe for yourself (Look for "Yourself"!). If you are lucky, you will see very clearly (perhaps briefly) that it is "your" tree, the tree is your consciousness, your consciousness is out there. That will seem quite weird and most people become frightened and deny the perception immediately before acknowledging it. In the same situation, let us look within instead. What do you sense there? Nothing? Indeed, there is only the tree *outside*, constituting your experience (except when your thoughts start wandering off or you look at the other trees nearby, etc). Neither looking out nor within, there is nothing else than the tree, the "subjective" "object", the subject/object. And definitely not a separate object and separate subject (looking at it). Neither has any independent existence, there is only one, unified experience or happening. It is not an external material object, nor an internal subjective experiencer/observer. It is just a single, conscious happening. Just consciousness.

We shall see that this sort of unified experience/happening not only applies to the perception of the external world, but likewise to the internal, mental world (thoughts, feelings, images, and intentions, whatever). *In neither case is there any separate observer, nor any separate object.*

We may think, believe, imagine, infer, pretend – there is an observer, but there is not. Hence the believing is an illusion (sometimes relating to the believed object, sometimes to the believed subject/observer/doer).

If the notion of an independent observer/doer, the Ego, is an illusion, the consequences are far-reaching, to put it mildly. We shall have to question all our taken-for-granted conceptions about free will, effort, self improvement, control, responsibility, fear/anxiety, aggression, morality. That is exactly what Zen suggests: no more. no less.

We are so accustomed to believing in and trusting, the central I, the Ego, the Me – that no one is willing to let it go. One of the reasons is that this "one" is the Ego itself, which foremost interest is to sustain itself at any cost (!). So the Ego will never be willing nor able to let go of itself. Consequently, liberation is not an act of will or good intentions or practice. The task is not to get rid of the Ego, but to see – not only theoretically, but experiencing beyond doubt – that the Ego does not really exist, except as a mental belief, the Big Misunderstanding. All the other Principles of Zen are pointers to help us understand and then experience the non-existence of the Ego and thus liberate our natural confidence in spontaneous awareness. This liberated state is what we called "Liberation" in the figure, or "Living the world", or "Spontaneous awareness". It seems impossible to find a label which is not also misleading. The best attempt so far is perhaps the 2,000 year-old "Tao", the name-less.

There are a lot of very clever descriptions of the Ego/Egoless-ness dilemma in Zen literature. The varieties may be more or less suitable according to personal preferences and are therefore worthwhile to pursue on an individual basis. [8,10,13,19,20,53,75,76,97,10 5,106,117,128,155]

NO DOING

If there is no Ego – and there isn't – there is neither a subject nor an object. If there is no subject, there is no Doer (nor a Victim). No Doer is one of the most contrary items as compared to common sense. We are so engaged in the feeling (and thinking) of being an active agent, pursuing goals, overcoming obstacles, achieving success. This is very close to the Ego-feeling of having expectations, making plans, taking decisions. While Ego is related to the mental life, No Doing is related to *actions*, or interaction with the environment (the social as well as the physical environment). Fortunately, everyone has regular contact with own actions as non-doing, actions happening by themselves. It is only when we *think* about it, that the active Doer appears. Again we are exposed to the (thinking) trap where we see ourselves apparently from the outside, as an agent acting upon its surroundings. Looking from within, we experience ourselves acting spontaneously and directly in the environment. Or re-acting upon changes happening to us. It is a unified organism/environment field. The dichotomy appears only during imagining. Unfortunately we do a lot imagining. The reason is that we do not trust ourselves; we have to constantly check upon our actions, re-decide, re-act, improve, and try something else. This nervous insecurity hinders the spontaneous flow of actions, makes us unpredictable for others and provokes insecurity in them too. If they respond with deliberate, disrupted action in return, we have a vicious circle where everybody keeps the others on tiptoe, being too much alert, too talkative, too smart, too serious, too much on guard, or too aggressive. [24,49,155] Deliberate Doing is like pulling yourself up by your own bootstraps. You can try, and you can believe it is necessary. Afterwards you may well believe that you succeeded thanks to the great effort and determination you put into it. (It is like snapping your fingers in order to keep pink elephants away. It works, no elephants!). Modern society has plenty of faith in effort, attributing success to effort, attributing failure to lack of effort. Zen is not advocating laissez-faire and laziness, which would be just another kind of belief/attitude. The point is rather that proper actions are taken naturally (when planned) or happen spontaneously (in the case of immediate interaction). The willed, forced effort is extra, superfluous and neurotic. [9,18,21,32,33,44,65,105,106,123,133]

Exercise

Take the opportunity to watch how much of your daily actions are spontaneous, i.e. happening more or less by themselves. Walking towards the door, opening it, closing it. Driving a car.

Sometimes you are aware of an intention, sometimes not even that.

On the other hand, also observe when you are deliberate; thinking about what to do or not to do, planning, being in doubt, making up your mind, deciding, changing your mind, forced acting, adjusting. Of course, there is a time for thinking and planning and deliberate adjustments. But not as a general mode of functioning. A good exercise is to experiment with making fewer plans or no plans for the day – and see what happens. You will probably end up doing more than usually. If you are tired and reluctant to embark on the daily "tasks", try sitting or lying relaxed for some time and see if the initiative shows up by itself. Routine tasks are typically performed much more easily when done in a state of "non-doing". It is somewhat more challenging to carry out more complex actions in the same mood of effortlessness, but it works. Just by observing yourself, being aware, you will notice if you are strenuous, and by itself you will gradually become more relaxed. Many people are not aware of the stressful manner in which they work or behave, wasting their own energy as well as others. [52]

To be very deliberate about relaxation, only adds to the superfluous effort. There are however, many good relaxation techniques that are more effective and better described than here. Our concern is not primarily with relaxation as such. For us it is more important as an indicator of the right way of acting, just as discomfort is an indication of fearful avoidance behaviour. The traditional basic exercise of Zen is to sit in meditation and quieten the mind: zazen, sitting zen. A great guide on Zen meditation is "The Art of Contemplation" (Alan Watts, 1972). [137] Most kinds of meditation techniques are very useful for revealing how full of stress we usually are and how unnecessary it is to stay that way. [32,47,48,64,69,71,72,73,74]

NO RESISTANCE

As there is no Ego, there is no Subject and no Object. No Subject implies no Doer, as we have seen. No Object implies no external actor/enforcer, no independent outer force making impact on us. We are not shuffled around by external forces causing us to do this and that. Or against which we have to defend ourselves. Whatever characteristics there are apparently external to the organism, they appear in our world only through (and as) the unified field which is our consciousness. What seems to happen "to" us is actually what happens. Just as we were no active (independent) Doer, we are no passive, independent Victim of external circumstances. Most people however, *believe* in an independent, external world (material and social) and consequently think and feel it necessary to be on guard and defend themselves. The result is a kind of paranoia where we disown or deny, that part of the environment which we do not like. And since this environment really is ourselves, we deny or disown ourselves – to a lesser or greater degree. On the surface we think we are properly critical of other people, or at least of their behaviour, if they are different from "us". Actually we are judgemental and project our dislikes on them.

This applies to almost all perceived differences between "me" and "them": from blunt racism to religious preferences to political opinions to physical and social differences to individual behaviour of what is considered "right" or "wrong".

But hey, certainly not all perceptions or opinions are judgemental? The answer is spontaneously given whenever you are able to perceive "what is" with no interference of "what should be".

If you yourself are under attack, you are the Victim. If you are attacking, you are the Critic or Controller. Both imply aggression and fear. And constriction of own and others freedom of opportunities. This attempted rejection (or denial) of dislikeable parts of our experience immediately backfires since we are really rejecting and disowning ourselves. The solution is simple to state, but harder to realise in everyday life: NO RESISTANCE!

There are two very peculiar implications here. The first is that there is a natural, spontaneous interaction "between" the "organism" and the "environment". The quotation marks signify that the concepts are not really independent entities, labelling them with separate words is misleading. The point is that there *is* a given happening in the organism/environment field. Both the "Stimulus" and the "Response" have already been taken care of. *Then* – and this is the second implication – we feel obliged to interfere because there are certain aspects of the happening (attributed to the object, environment) which we do not like. This is the Resistance. We want to change the input, deny it or move away from it. The important implication here is that this Resistance is intentional, willed, a choice. It is a deliberate action or response to the original happening, rejecting it. And since the first spontaneous action is ourselves (and not an alien object in the environment), we are rejecting ourselves in self denial. The good news is that this Resistance is our own *action*, so if we just refrain from doing it, spontaneity is non-interrupted! Which is what it's all about. With this intellectual knowledge about Dislike, Resistance and No Resistance, we are more likely to discover and become aware of such situations in everyday life. The feeling of discomfort associated with negative events or people – especially the expectation and imagining of such events – is generally a helpful sign indicating your Resistance to the situation. By becoming aware of your Resistance, you re-own the complete situation and the perception of a "problem" disappears. Things may still need adjustments or adaptations, but they are not alienated (disowned, denied) or experienced as personal problems any longer. [3,4,44,77,80,81,114,128]

Exercise

One dramatic variant of Resistance is the one of being mildly depressed, feeling low. This is a kind of rejection of yourself, being disappointed with yourself. When you then try to "pull yourself together", it usually doesn't work; it is like pulling yourself up by your bootstraps again. Perhaps you even get worse because you receive yet more proof that you are worthless or failing. If however, you are lucky and observant and self accepting, you may suddenly discover (become aware of) that you are *making* yourself unhappy, that you are *acting* depressed intentionally. In that sense, you are wanting, creating, the depressive feeling. In the split second you discover that, the depressive feeling vanishes into thin air. You can make yourself feel miserable and then pretend that you can't help it, but you cannot act and pretend helplessness at the same time. There are limits to how much we can fool ourselves. Fortunately.

NO IMPROVEMENT (OF ONESELF)

As there is no independent Doer, nor is there any Doer to be improved upon. The fundamental dualism of subject and object implies a basic distrust, both towards the subject (person) and towards the object (external world). Distrusting the subject means that you are never sure whether you are acting right, doing the right things in the right way. You hesitate and worry before acting, you check and change your mind while acting, and you regret your behaviour after acting. Then you start being more systematic about your distrust and plan your "self improvement". That is usually a lifelong journey for those who start travelling along this path. The number of self improvement techniques, schools and traditions has never been in shortage, but is now exploding. If one method does not work, try harder, or try a better technique, or meet my guru, etc. The bad news is: working on yourself will never work. It is the bootstrap fallacy again. A case of the blind leading the blind. Even worse: there is no one to govern nor to be governed, because the active subject wasn't there in the first place. The improvement ideology is perhaps the most ardent one in contemporary common sense (in Western and modern Eastern countries). We will not let it go easily. Its reputation is glorified. Often it is regarded as being more virtuous to try to learn and improve than to act and behave properly in the first place. The competition between the beliefs and techniques effectively overshadows the common dubious improvement philosophy. Development or improvement is really one of the cherished gods of our time. The potential gain by disclosing it is correspondingly great.

Exercise

The discomfort and feeling of inadequacy of the Ego makes it most logical, almost inevitable, to strive for the improvement of oneself. Since this is a self-defeating enterprise, the result will be disappointment and only add to the frustration or even despair for those most addicted. Advice no. 1 is to take this (theoretical) hint that all your striving is in the wrong direction, and secondly, to test for yourself what happens when you dare to let go of your improvement projects, one after another. Start with one simple "should" by which you try to improve yourself. Tell yourself that this "should" is itself an obstacle for change. If you really want to do something differently, just do it. Trying is lying.[72,74,77,83,154]

NO CONTROL

The Ego distrusts the external world because it feels alienated in the relationship. It is a kind of paranoia, feeling somewhat isolated in surroundings which are not-me and are perceived as more or less threatening. If not being controlled. We figure we have to safeguard against a potential danger or at least, cultivate the environment to our liking, make it ours. Without due regard for the beauty and intelligence of natural habitats as such, we are apt to exploit our environment rather than nurture it. This goes for the social environment as well as for the physical one. At the lowest, most material level, things are perceived as "good" or "bad", and we act accordingly towards them. We act to enhance the good ones and eliminate the bad ones; join the good guys and fight the bad guys. At another stage, we engage ourselves somewhat more, get more involved with the environment, and act to change it. The focus is then on right or wrong and we are more ethically concerned.

Exercise

The inclination to control the environment, especially other people, has of course far-reaching consequences and does not necessarily coincide with the wishes of other people in general, and of those being controlled, in particular. (!)

Just because everybody's intentions are so good (apparently), these activities are not easily revealed. But for now we are focusing on our own self-discovery where we are actively and curiously looking for surprises and hidden truths about ourselves. An aggressive, hostile or urgent emotion, so often accompanying a controlling behaviour, is a sure sign that the action is really a kind of violation. If so, follow your heart, not your worried head. Beware of all the shoulds, should nots, musts and must nots. "The preoccupation with right and wrong, is the sickness of the mind". [8,9,132] "Grant to others that which you want for yourself". [44,71,74]

When the object of control is oneself rather than the external world, the same warnings apply. Self-hate is as devastating as it is common. Control towards oneself may be described as a variant of trying to improve, and therefore also relevant to the previous discussion of "No Improvement". [1,44,85,109]

NO THINKING

Thinking is worrying. Rational thinking is of course THE human faculty per se. It enables us to categorize, imagine, analyse, predict, plan, learn, communicate and transfer knowledge between each other and between generations. It covers everything from fleeting thoughts to collective cultural understanding about ourselves and the universe. Thinking is for most people the highlight of the personal, conscious, deliberate way of coping with ourselves and the world. Thinking is problem-solving, our own way of becoming aware of new combinations of concepts. Thinking is close to the ego-feeling of control, mental observation, choices and free will. Myself as the problem solver thinking thoughts. However, how much of your daily "streams of consciousness" is really useful problem-solving or necessary planning? You may solve a task at work or plan the shopping list in your head. But mostly we rely on routine work and know what to do. However, "the stream of consciousness" goes on incessantly. The inner chatter, the small talk to ourselves, never stops and produces nothing. It is excessive verbalization, inner talking, commenting, predicting, judging – especially about what has happened before or what might happen in the future. This is mostly worrying. Don't buy the idea that it is necessary and rational.

Exercise

Observe and test this out. Everyone has plenty of examples to become aware of. You may even have adopted the strategy that you should worry long before the events are coming up – to be on the safe side – so you don't get disappointed if things don't go your way. Or you meticulously prepare details which are better taken care of on the spur of the moment in the actual social setting. Or you avoid being prepared, when you should have been, just to avoid the nervous preparation period or to pretend that you are carefree. Everyone has certain "themes", major issues which they worry about from the past or for the future. These may waste a lot of energy and arrest well-being.

Thinking is a kind of Resistance to the external world, an attempt to avoid unpleasant events.

Unfortunately these events are also part of ourselves, they are not really external. Although thinking appears in the guise of problem solving, it is a kind of attempt to escape. When the whole situation is embraced, the feeling of fear disappears. The Ego pretends that it is thinking the thoughts, but there is only thinking, or rather, only thoughts. And the thoughts are often fear in disguise. When the fear is observed and acknowledged, there is no more need to run away and the "problem" changes into a "task" or a plain fact to be naturally accepted. [27,44,50,54,74,101,137]

NO AVOIDANCE

Just as Thinking may be a kind of Resistance to the perceived external world, so may physical Avoidance be a strategy to attain the same ends. Thinking is avoidance of imagined events, while physical Avoidance is a retreat from actual situations. "No problem is so great that you cannot run away from it". Is that actually true? The very act of escaping will often turn out to be the problem itself. As before, the situation which we want to avoid is really a part of ourselves, and the avoidance is therefore trying to run away from oneself, a kind of escapism. To retreat is often a defeat without really trying, your "reward" is that you avoid the experience of defeat by not really participating.

Exercise

See if you can recognize any of these examples from your own life. Physical avoidance may take many forms. These include not showing up to a meeting or to a party, refraining from stressful events or tasks, hiding or down-playing our own opinions in discussions, avoiding certain people, avoiding commitments, not keeping appointments, not making appointments until the last minute. A variant is to wholly refrain from participation or involvement. Or to deny that one is interested. To participate or stay in the situation, but with fear, is no optimal solution either, although the anxiety may be reduced over time if the situation is repetitive. Examples might be giving speeches, giving lectures, and the like. The clue is to embrace the whole situation and experience what is generating the fear or rather why and how *you are creating* the fear. [27,28,72,73]

SPONTANEITY

The Zen Principles described so far are all No's: don't do this or that, or rather stop doing, stop resisting, stop controlling, stop pretending. The clue is that this is all we really need to "do", the un-doing of fighting or defending against a perceived, fictional alien world. Then the natural functioning takes over, no additional measures are necessary. But what happens then? Who knows? (Who cares?). Nobody knows, that's the thrill of it. In most cases people may still go to the same jobs, have the same interests as before, etc. But *the way of doing things* will be different, being more relaxed, more engaged, more joyful. And a lot of unnecessary limitations, frustrations and fears may release a potential for new activities. Not necessarily happiness, not necessarily un-neurotic, definitely not a rose garden, perhaps not even a "nice" personality (by whose standards?). Acting naturally means exactly that, acting in accordance with natural endowments, experience and circumstances. Not according to more or less contemporary beliefs, expectations or misunderstandings. Whether they are self-imposed or imprinted upon you by your family or socio-cultural context. Anti-beliefs and anti-rules are of course just another kind of self-imposed constrictions and are no liberation. The solution is definitely not anarchy, nor hedonism, selfishness or laissez-faire. But free consciousness, willingly and playfully doing and

experiencing whatever happens when being fully present (with all of "you", here and now, at any time). This is the principle of Spontaneity. It is not an obligation or instruction to be followed, but at most a tacit intention or awareness, a freedom which you allow yourself (and others!). If Spontaneity is planned as a goal in itself, it vanishes – immediately. It is thus easily corrupted. Trust yourself, you are inherently and un-escapable spontaneous, in every moment. It only doesn't look like it when you are *trying* to take control (of yourself or the environment). There is only NOW, in moment after moment after moment.
2,5,6,9,32,116,128,157

Exercise

Spontaneous versus forced motivation.

When you are ill you have an excellent opportunity to observe your varying degree of "motivation", energy, initiative. It could be some minor illness, a flu, for example, or a more serious one. Most of us have a large number of smaller or bigger obligations which still should be dealt with regardless of the need for rest and recovery. Some bills should be paid, mail read and responded to, plans have to be made along with some phone calls, etc. Observe two things:

1. Your inner voice and concern telling you that you "should" take care of these tasks or perhaps postpone them somewhat, etc.

2. Your lack of "motivation" and initiative, corresponding to your state of well-being (or ill-being).

3. Your increase of "motivation" when you gradually become better. Notice that the moralising is unnecessary and does not improve the "motivation" at all. This is contrary to the strong common sense imperative to "pull yourself together". The energy increases spontaneously and corresponds with

your recovery. No more motivation is needed, things are just being done.

The significance of this observation depends on actually experiencing it and understanding that it contradicts the common sense of moralising. Remember to transfer the insight to your everyday confusion about "motivation and duties", about "should's and want's". Trusting your natural engagement is even more important during your well-being as during ill-being because you are harder on yourself when you are well.

Notice all the Spontaneous activities in your daily life. Observe it, *appreciate* it, and learn from it. You are the best model (guru!) when things are going well and likewise you provide a bad but useful case when you are confused.

Spontaneity is the subjective aspect of Liberation. The objective aspect is Acceptance.

ACCEPTANCE

When there is no Resistance to the external world, there is Acceptance. This is also a kind of un-doing or no-doing, in the sense that letting go of Resistance is all that is needed, the Acceptance works by itself. Indeed, just as for Spontaneity, there is a fallacy in trying to be deliberately Accepting. It immediately becomes corrupted. Forced Acceptance is like trying to be good, trying to be tolerant – with the self-contradicting implication and projection that there is something bad out there which requires your acceptance (apropos ethics). True Acceptance is much more fundamental, inherent and definitely not imposed, neither from others nor yourself. Acceptance is the natural way of functioning when we don't try to interfere. In fact, it is so natural and fundamental that we cannot really avoid it; we can only try or pretend that we are not being accepting. This requires a few more words.

Since the subject/object split is only an imagined dualism, the world (our world, your world) is not really external to you, it is THE world or the me/world (me-world). It is all there is, just happening. The question about Accepting only arises if you want to reject some part of this happening (because you dislike it). Whether you try to Resist it or not, the happening is as it is, you have already "accepted" (perceived) it in the first place. Sorry, too late for not Accepting it; you are only entitled to try to Resist and protest and make a lot of fuss about it afterwards, confusing yourself (and others) by disowning what is happening to you.

Spontaneity implies there is nothing wrong with me. [74,75]

Acceptance implies "loving what is". [79]

Exercise

Observe yourself while listening to, looking at, or talking with people you more or less dislike. See if you can perceive them without the negative verbal labels. People on TV may also function as examples. Perception with no judgements. Another example is where you now actually perceive the person or situation acceptingly, although you once reacted with disgust. Learning from your own spontaneous behaviour is as good a guru as any. It is in fact the best one. It is the only one. [44,74,79,111,113]

LIBERATION

If the "principles" of Spontaneity and Acceptance are not instructions to be followed or acted upon deliberately, this applies even more to the final result of Liberation. This state or way of being or way of happening is so all-encompassing and so intangible that it is best left unnamed. Any labelling (and even worse, any instructions) delimits, deceives, and misses the immanent or basic life force, or whatever we may call it. And why not? There is no reason that such a fundamental "phenomenon" should be describable in words at all. Historically, quite a few good terms have been proposed to hint at this essence: Tao, the Name-less, the Unspeakable, Void, going with the flow, pure consciousness, Consciousness is all, Love, Loving What Is, Nature, God, It, Stillness, Reality, Enlightenment, bliss, Is-ness, being.

A question mark (?) or an exclamation mark (!) are not bad names either, if you can appreciate open answers. If we renounce our obsession with describing, explaining and understanding, we perhaps get nearer: "it is closer than your own breath". [102,103,110] "It is so close that we overlook it". It is What you are. It is Who you are. It is Us. It is It. It Is. It. Is. ?!

Nevertheless, as shown in the Figure "Zen Psychology in a Nutshell", we have chosen the keyword "Liberation" or "Living the World" (being and creating, as one and the same happening). This is meant to combine two sides of the now united man/nature (organism/environment, person/world). The one side is the apparent passive Acceptance of What Is (being in the world). The other side is the apparent active Spontaneity of creating the World (realising the world). As in the symbol for Tao (signifying the name-less), these paradoxes are reconciled in one harmonious entity:

When regarded separately, as most people are inclined to do, you are left with one side mistaken as genuinely passive where the world pushes you around. The other side is mistaken as genuinely active where you push the world around. Both halves imply a split and confrontation between you and the world. Attempts at re-conciliation can never succeed (!) for the simple reason that you assume a Me and not-Me from the very start. As long as this split is not transcended, no technique, no therapy, no New Age will help us. The frustration may only increase. This is the sorrow of the human mind. And it has been with us for some time.

Our so-called rational or logical thinking is more limited and primitive than we would like to believe. For one thing, we believe everything may be thought, said or written in words, those arbitrary, linear, virtual units which at best point to a representation (mental picture) of the real world. But even at the verbal level we are inclined to use the simplest form of labelling. For instance, we prefer "either/or" (this or that) when there are several alternatives. "Both" is more complicated, so is "neither/nor". Even more advanced is the interconnected-ness of polar, but co-existent opposites, like good/bad, winner/loser, success/failure, happy/unhappy, fortunate/unfortunate, ardent/ lazy, rich/poor. These items are dependant on and relative to each other. Yet we tend to treat them as absolute values and cling to their positive value as if that were possible in real life. We build a virtual reality, a shadow world of concepts which are inherently artificial and contradicting. The result is frustration when the world does not "deliver". "We can all be winners and everyone should do their best". (If not, they are suckers). "Everyone has free will, if he or she really wants to". "Everyone can and should improve themselves". "Everyone can stay healthy if they really want to".

Exercise

Look if you can recognise similar "shoulds" or "should nots" in the society, among family and friends or perhaps yourself.

On a more advanced level we discover that the very question/ problem itself is wrong and represents a misunderstanding. And this is required for all the main issues that are radical to common sense. That's why they are perceived as radical and that's why they provide substantial development. They are not necessarily complex and may well be seen as self evident afterwards, that is, after a change of mind. [3,7,8,26,34,43,44,49,60,101,114]

This is exactly what we shall discover in the next chapter. [3,6,8,26,35,46,47,54,69]

CHAPTER 5

COMMON ZENSE

ZEN PSYCHOLOGY APPLIED TO COMMON SENSE AND EVERYDAY LIFE

INTRODUCTION: ZEN AND COMMON SENSE

The following 51 themes from everyday life represent life situations, or problems, we all share. They are firmly rooted in our common sense but are here reviewed in the light of Zen Psychology. While the "10 pillars of Zen" are a combination of Zen and Psychology, the 51 themes are a combination of Zen and Common sense. It is Zen applied to common life situations or challenges. The reader may well choose and pick particular themes of interest. The sequence is not critical, but it is expected that the items will progress from easy to more difficult to understand. As we shall see later, this progression corresponds to several levels of perception, each level representing a characteristic perspective (viewpoint) on the world and oneself. As a reader you will later be invited to "test" yourself as to your most prevalent perspective. The concept is that the way of perceiving the world is at the same time a reflection (projection) of ones personal state of mind, or rather, there is no difference between the two, they are one and the same.

51 CHALLENGES IN EVERYONES LIFE

DUALISM CHALLENGES

1. DUALISM

If you feel there is a strong division between yourself and the world around you, you are probably at the dualistic level of consciousness development (or in a current life crisis which pulls you back to this level temporarily). Your person (ego) may seem strong or weak according to how successful you are, but the world will be very much painted in black and white with Good Guys and Bad Guys, Right or Wrong, Justice and Injustice. Your closest ally is your ego, which you feel should expand whenever there is opportunity, and be defended whenever threatened. Since the outer world is alien, it should be controlled and not trusted. Conflicts are thriving and look natural and unavoidable, at this stage. [62,63,159]

At a more advanced level (the humanistic one) one tries to improve the world and other people. Later on again (it may be many years or centennials later), one may suspect that something is wrong also with this external idealism. We discover that others may be equally convinced in pursuing their idealistic goals which may be quite opposed to ours. Or we may easily see that sometimes, or often, their idealistic engagement is really motivated by quite egoistic interests. Or we may discover our own egoistic motives. Furthermore, the expected positive results are not that obvious. Gradually one starts to question the motivation of the ego. One starts to want egoless-ness, to be more objective, less selfish, and preferably even self-less. This is the seeking of true altruism. Later on, even altruism itself will be questioned. One becomes more self-improvement oriented rather than improving the external world. Later still, the scepticism towards improvement is also applied to oneself. That's when true Seeking really begins.

Zen saying

"This points to the connection between intellect and physical sensation: Concepts lead to sensations, and therefore, false concepts lead to illusions. We have seen this principle demonstrated before with all kinds of optical illusions. In those illusions our *concept* influences our *sensation.* A central point in Zen is that we have a concept of our own existence and of the world which is fallacious, and Zen will help us get rid of that concept so that we will have a new sensation. People get worried when they hear this and say, "Well, are we just going to exchange one hallucination for another?" Let me respond with a question or two: How do you know when you know that you know? What is the *test* of "truth" about something that you "feel"? You may say, "Well, I can feel that I'm Napoleon, or that I'm being persecuted by the government." But this is an hallucination, even though one might feel it very strongly. In our culture, we have a "test" of truth which is science. We say, "If something can be demonstrated scientifically, then we're inclined to believe that it's not an hallucination." All right, let's go along with that. I think this is rather relative, but I will always in any argument grant the premises of the person who wants to argue with me, and take it from there. Let's assume that sciences like biology and physics are ways of discovering the "truth." When we grant that, we find that the hallucination of being a separate ego will not stand up to biological tests! From the point of view of biology, the individual organism is in the same "behaviour system" as the environment, and in fact the organism and the environment constitute a single system of behaviour which is neither deterministic nor voluntary. The two are really one activity, and they call it the "field of the organism-environment." Ecology is the study of these kinds of fields." (Alan Watts: What is Zen?) [153]

2. STRESS

The stress or tension you experience at any time, reflects your own state of mind as well as the objective situation "itself". How much it depends on your own understanding, is for you to find out. The result will surprise you, shake you or shock you. And it will become a vital motivation for going on in your investigations.

At the stage of "Dualism" there is a profound feeling of separateness. The Good is pitted against the Evil, the Good Guys against the Bad Guys. There is fundamentalism and confrontation. The world is to be saved and primarily through fighting the immoral "others". This goes for all kinds of issues, whether related to politics, religion, nationality, race or gender. Are there any instances of such confrontations in the world of today? Or is this kind of consciousness belonging to a more primitive culture way back in history....

Zen saying

"It is important when we are encountering restlessness to expand our awareness to the unacknowledged feeling or emotion beneath the obsessive thoughts. The fact that we have not faced the anxiety or the guilt is what allows it to escalate into restlessness. Our task is to drop below the level of the repetitive thoughts and, mindfully and compassionately, experience what we are actually feeling. This way we experience both relief and release, going beyond a habitual relationship to our pain. Ironically, we can even be filled with a great sense of comfort in the midst of pain. This is happiness that arises not from what is happening to us, but from how we are relating to what is happening to us. We are relating to our feelings with the inner knowledge, "It is okay. I do not have to run; I do not have to push the pain away. I do not have to get lost in it. It is okay to simply be aware of it." This quality of relating openly to our feelings is the antidote for restlessness, guilt, and anxiety. When we develop the ability to open to our underlying feelings, we can transform guilt into wise remorse. Being aware of whatever we are experiencing with a peaceful attitude allows us not to be driven into restlessness."

(Sharon Salzberg: A Heart as wide as the World) [114]

3. FEAR

The "reality" you are experiencing is reflecting a certain stage in the development of consciousness. For instance, the conflicts, anxiety, fear, worry, inhibitions, are not real in an objective sense, they are your perceptions, your world, at this stage. At the level of "Humanism", there is a partly insight in this perspective of relative reality: there is a certain feeling and need for community, communication, sharing, compromises, different perspectives, trying to be tolerant of people or systems which do not correspond directly with your view. This is a great step beyond direct confrontation (the level of "Dualism").

However, unwillingly you find yourself thrown into conflicts. Why? Because there are limits to what you believe to be acceptable or non-threatening. At this stage you try to discuss matter rather than person, trying to be objective, trying to adapt and interact. There is a tentative understanding of unity with people and Nature, but only when we do not feel threatened. This stage is characterised by wanting to improve the world and other people.

Zen saying

"Sometimes we are afraid to open to something painful because it seems as though it will consume us. Yet the nature of mindfulness is that it is never overcome by whatever is the present object of awareness. If we are mindful of a twisted or distorted state of mind, the mindfulness is not twisted or distorted. Even the most painful state of mind or the most difficult feeling in the body does not ruin mindfulness. A true opening, born of mindfulness, is marked by spaciousness and grace. In our culture we are taught to push away, to avoid our feelings. This kind of aversion is the action of a mind caught in separation. Whether in the active, fiery form of anger and rage, or in a more inward, frozen form like fear, the primary function of these mental states is to separate us from what we are experiencing. But the only way that we can be free from suffering ourselves and avoid doing harm to others is by connection, a connection to our own pain and, through awareness and compassion, a connection to the pain of others. We learn not to create separation from anything or anyone. This is empathy." (Sharon Salzberg: A Heart as wide as the World) [114]

4. AGGRESSION

Beware not to project your problems into the world. Observe yourself carefully. Stop trying to save or improve others or the world. Help others when a good opportunity offers itself, it is a natural, self-evident kind of reaction of being human. Helping or supporting is natural. Whenever it is felt as an obligation, desire or ambition, you should check your motives. You may find that you are somehow doing it for your own interests. Is the help really wanted? Are there no strings attached? Are you condescending? Is others misery a comfort for you? You are not supposed to be "Gods little helper" (D.E.Harding: Head off stress). [56]

Zen saying

"Whenever the energy of anger comes up, we often want to express it to punish the person whom we believe to be the source of our suffering. This is the habit of energy in us. When we suffer, we always blame the other person for having made us suffer. We do not realize that anger is, first of all, our business. We are primarily responsible for our anger, but we believe very naively that if we can say something or do something to punish the other person, we will suffer less. This kind of belief should be uprooted. Because whatever you do or say in a state of anger will only cause more damage in the relationship. Instead, we should try not to do anything or say anything when we are angry. When you say something really unkind, when you do something in retaliation, your anger increases. You make the other person suffer, and he will try hard to say or do something back to get relief from his suffering. That is how the conflict escalates. This has happened so many times in the past. You are both very familiar with the escalation of anger, of suffering, and yet you have not learned anything from it. Trying to punish the other person is only going to make the situation worse. Punishing the other person is self-punishment. That is true in every circumstance." (Thich Nhat Hanh: Anger) [49]

5. DEPRESSION

Almost all thinking is worrying!

This is not for accepting or rejecting in an abstract way. Try it out for yourself, observe yourself, take your time. If you don't believe you are worried, try to stop the noisy chatter that is going on all the time inside your head. Be absolutely calm, just be aware. You'll find that you are not able to, you are too worried (unless you use meditation techniques or are very advanced). When you get in touch with the worrying nature of thought, be careful not to condemn yourself, not to condemn the worries. Accept them, observe them as they are, and they will gradually lose their power and fade away. *Be nice to yourself*. The reason you were (more or less) depressed in the first place, is often because you condemn yourself for worrying, for not being strong enough. That's a vicious circle which turns worry into depression. Start with accepting the depression then, if that's how you feel. Always start accepting yourself, be kind (!). This leads to insight, which leads to freedom. If you are very lucky, you may even discover that you in fact *want* to be depressed, that it is willed (!). In that instance, it disappears immediately.

When you are very worried about something in particular (taking a test, exam, appointment, party, meeting, make a speech- whatever) is often a good opportunity for learning. In that case, you may observe your worrying which is very distinct. Then deliberately *allow* yourself not to worry. Do not *try* to stop worrying, just allow yourself not to worry (the worrying is your own doing in the first place as it is in every moment). But be aware: worrying is a very, very strongly engrained habit. It is the most common form of self-hate and your ego is most expert in that game.

Zen saying

"I suspect we focus on "learning from our mistakes" (beating ourselves up over them) because that keeps us from paying attention to what we are doing NOW.

Remember, as long as you are out of the moment, self-hate is in control."

(Cheri Huber: There Is Nothing Wrong With You for TEENS) [74]

6. CONFLICT WITH THE WORLD

You and others and Nature are one. It is a profound and dangerous myth that you are a separate independent entity from Nature or the world around you. The myth makes you feel lonely, defensive and even hostile towards the environment (both physical and social environment). Not because you are bad, but because you are afraid and feel alienated. The same goes for the others around you, of course. Your paranoia will thrive on real threats in addition to the imagined ones. ("Being paranoid doesn't mean nobody is stalking you").

It helps to see how anxious the others are, that makes them less mean, easier to tolerate.

Observe the physical world, the wall in the room, the trees outside. Are they not part of your consciousness? Are they not your consciousness? Are they not *you*? Are *they* filling your consciousness, or are *you* making them conscious? Does it matter? The result is there/here. It also goes for your personal environment, the person you believe is facing you, confronting you. In time you'll see this unity directly. It has radical consequences, but all in due time.

Zen saying

"In sum, then, the realization that nature is ordered organically rather than politically, that it is a field of relationships rather than a collection of things, requires an appropriate mode of human awareness. The habitual egocentric mode in which man identifies himself with a subject facing a world of alien objects does not fit the physical situation. So long as it remains, our inward feeling is at variance with reality. Based on this feeling, our efforts to control ourselves and the surrounding world become viciously circular entanglements of ever-growing complexity. More and more the individual feels himself frustrated and impotent in the midst of a mechanical world order which has become an irresistible "march of progress" toward ends of its own. Therapies for the frustrated individual, whether religious or psychological, merely complicate the problem in so far as they assume that the separate ego is the very reality toward which their ministrations are directed. For, as Trigant Burrow saw, the source of the trouble is social rather than individual: that is to say, the ego is a social convention foisted upon human consciousness by conditioning. The root of mental disorder is not therefore a malfunctioning peculiar to this or that ego; it is rather that the ego-feeling as such is an error of perception. To placate it is only to enable it to go on confusing the mind with a mode of awareness which, because it clashes with the natural order, breeds the vast family of psychological frustrations and illnesses. An organic natural order has its proper correspondence in a mode of consciousness which is a total feeling or experiencing. Where feeling is broken up into the feeler and the feeling, the knower and the known, what lies between the two is not relationship, but mere juxtaposition. Identified with one of its terms alone, consciousness feels "out on a limb" facing an alien world which it controls only to find it more and more uncontrollable, and which it exploits only to find it more and more un-gratifying." (Alan W. Watts: Nature, Man and Woman) [136]

7. RELIGION/PSYCHOLOGY/POLITICS

All "belief systems", whether religion, psychology or politics, are based on the concept of an objective common world described by some fundamental "truths". This applies even or especially, to our Common Sense, which covers all we take for granted and therefore least subjected to inquiry and testing. [61,62,64,87,127,132,133]

Good and Bad news:

You believe in an "objective" world out there, separate from yourself which is described as a subject observing the objects.

This is a most workable basis of natural science. Even more important, it is taken for granted as part of common sense, at least in the industrial cultures. However, this perspective may not be as true as it looks. For one thing, the dualistic view separates you from the outer world. Is that how you really perceive the world? Do you *observe* it or just see it as it is? If you observe it, you are out of your senses and into your head, sleep-walking. Moreover, you feel separated and alienated, which makes you frightened, defensive, selfish or aggressive. You may feel lost and confused, but do not know why.

That was the Bad News....

Now to the Good ones!

Later on you will discover that you never really were separated. There is nothing to be afraid of, the problems are virtual, it was "only" a nightmare.

For many people it may seem disrespectful (or worse) to question the validity of belief systems, especially the great religions and the belief in a personal God. However, there may exist an even nobler obligation or challenge, that is paying attention to What is, being totally and unconditionally present in the Here and Now. As different from escaping the present situation, denying our true Nature by pretending to be inferior or superior, worshipping abstract ideas and holy images, trading a constricted life on earth for an eternal one in heaven.

Zen saying

"The way of Religion.

If we look for help here to what goes by the name of religion, to religion as a social phenomenon, to religion as described and practiced by their majority of its adherents, to religion as dished out daily in the media, we shall surely look in vain. So far from clearing mists away, it piles up the pollution and obscurity. As for its history, religion has been responsible for more inhumanity, more pig-headedness, more fat-headedness, more terror, more fraud than any of the human undertaking.

Yet here is a case of the worst concealing the best. Common to the worlds great faiths is a Metaphysic – a wisdom, a spirituality, a secret and often the truly suppressed teaching – according to which, in spite of all appearances to the contrary, you and I and all creatures are, a Centre, not creatures at all, but One with their Creator. That at the core of all beings lurks Being Itself, the Nameless One whose nicknames Atman-Brahman, the Tao, god, the Indwelling Christ, the Holy Spirit, Allah, Reality, Consciousness, the No-thing that is Everything. This Metaphysic gives us two priceless pieces of information about the nameless One. We are told exactly *where* It is. And exactly what It is, exactly how we shall recognise It when at last we track it down.

According to Mohammed, it's nearer to me than the vein in my neck. According to Tennyson, it's nearer than my breathing, closer than hands and feet. Much, much closer, say all those who know what they are talking about.

"The very spot I am looking out of, the place I'm coming from, this Centrepoint, that is far more me than Harding is me – this is the Home, the royal palace of His Divine Majesty, say the world's great spiritual teachers."

1.   (Douglas E. Harding: "To Be and not to be, that is the answer") [60]

8. ZEN

It is easier to say what Zen is not. It is neither psychology, religion, philosophy nor politics. It is non-theoretical, a non-system. It is pro-Nature, pro-spontaneity, pro present moment living. It may be said to be a way of living or orientation towards what is experienced as a natural, non-forced way of perceiving the world, other persons and oneself. It cannot be described in words. One may only point or hint at it. Those who have insight, will understand the slightest sign. Those who have not, will not understand in a hundred years. If you are perceptive, there are signs everywhere, "closer than your own breath". Everyone has to start with himself or herself. Life itself gives feedback, in time. At a certain stage in the development of consciousness human beings become aware of their own self-consciousness and long for a return to their original, natural, spontaneous way of living, a bliss which everyone has enjoyed in childhood. Zen is not only anti-theoretical (though more neutralising than antagonistic), it is anti common sense. Your very most appreciated beliefs or values may thus be challenged. For instance, being an independent being with a personal ego courageously fighting against a threatening world and trying to improve the morality of fellow beings. In spite of all the confusion, tension and conflicts in the world, Zen is all-including and accepting, ensuring that all and everyone are really not deviating from the natural course of living. Life will provide feedback, in due time. You never really left Home. The nightmare may, however, be rather unpleasant before you finally wake up.

Zen saying

"Zen is a method of rediscovering the experience of being alive. It originated in India and China, and has come to the West by way of Japan, and although it is a form of Mahayana Buddhism, it is not a religion in the usual sense of the word. The aim of Zen is to bring about a transformation of consciousness, and to awaken us from the dream world of our endless thoughts so that we experience life as it is in the present moment. Zen cannot really be taught, but it can be transmitted through sessions of contemplation or meditation called *zazen,* and through dialogues between student and teacher, called *sanzen.* In the dialogue between the student and Zen master the student comes squarely up against the obstacles to his or her understanding and, without making the answer obvious, the master points a finger toward the way." (Mark Watts, Introduction) (Alan Watts: What is Zen?) [153]

9. GOOD/BAD

In Zen there are a lot of mystical pointers: There is no free will, Man is God, I am That (or It), and so are You; Who are you?; I am You, You are Me. A lot of concepts are turned upside down. *The devil* (if there is any) is linked to Thinking, with about just the opposite value as in common sense: self criticism, worrying, conscience. Thinking is further associated with comparisons, monitoring, control, "good" intentions, the conscious I, ego, morality, self "improvement". The positive side of the Devil/Thinking is being clever: focus, intelligence, change and challenges, solutions and learning.

"Angels" are your real Self, as expressed in spontaneity, perception, seeing what is, nature, play, love, unselfishness, nothingness, absentness, now. The devil and the angels will be recognised (as you), revealed, re-interpreted and accepted (as God in disguise). Angels will be discovered, recognised (as you), accepted as your "doing". The most vital things happen independently of what we believe in and strive for.

Zen saying

"It May Be True...

It may be true that you make sacrifices, but that doesn't make you good, it just means you make sacrifices.

It may be true that you are accepting, but that doesn't make you good, it just means you are accepting.

It may be true that you are responsible, but that doesn't make you good, it just means you are responsible.

It may be true that you don't take drugs, but that doesn't make you good, it just means you don't take drugs.

It may be true that you don't have sex, but that doesn't make you good, it just means you don't have sex.

It may be true that you don't say mean things, but that doesn't make you good, it just means you don't say mean things.

It may be true that you meditate, but that doesn't make you good, it just means you meditate.

We label these behaviours good and then continue to do them in order to support self-hate. Perhaps <u>doing</u> in order to be good is what keeps you from realizing that you are already good."

(Cheri Huber: There Is Nothing Wrong With You for TEENS)[74]

HUMANISM CHALLENGES

10. DISSATISFIED

Entangled in conscious, verbal opinions, we will always feel unsatisfied, because something is missing. And for good reasons.

Consciousness has a negative side. In order that something is focused on in awareness, something else has to become unfocused, like figure and ground, foreground and background.

One thing is conscious, another is unconscious, or at least neglected. Consciousness is very selective, myopic and focused on details. While awareness and perception are more oriented towards a totality, a full picture, a hands-on experience of the complete situation. This pre-conscious experience is more immediate, more perceptual, more total, less abstract, and less selective. In our culture we have come to extremely overestimate the value of myopic consciousness at the cost of the more direct perceptual form of awareness. We rely too much on language, beliefs and verbal constructions, too little on overall impressions, intuition, and immediate experience. The consciousness we adore represents verbalisations, prioritisations, choices, comparisons, change, control, intention, monitoring, focus, specialisations, and details. They are all clever, oh so clever, tools. They are useful, as long as they are seen as constructs and not realities, details and not complete. When they are mistaken for facts, as when they are believed in, we get lost in our own web of artificial abstractions.

We may spend a whole life striving for an abstract goal while forgetting the process, the being, which is the only real existence.

Zen saying

"Countless numbers of us have done therapy of one sort or another. We have taken seminars on subjects ranging from our wounded inner child to time management. We have invested time and money in everything from meditation retreats to walking on fire and high-energy effectiveness trainings. We have planned our days, changed our diets and visualized our goals. And yet, for the two of us, after attending hundreds of seminars and courses, and reading plenty of inspirational books, there was still a sense of emptiness. After each seminar, retreat or book, we would have a new system through which to view life. We would feel hyped up or enthusiastic about ourselves, sometimes even changed and revitalized, but sooner or later, we would be lying awake at night thinking, "There has got to be more to life than this." " (Ariel & Shya Kane: Working on Yourself Doesn't Work) [77]

11. BELIEF IN SYSTEMS

Why do we think we need something to believe in? Belief is doubt. Why don't we trust ourselves? Clinging to a system means that we distrust ourselves. Distrusting ourselves is not a virtue, it is a vice. The same goes for distrusting other people. Distrusting is almost like planning to fail. Trying is lying.

Here is the Bad News:

Acceptance means also the negative aspects, whatever you deem them to be, *especially* the negative aspects, in you and in others. The devil, if there is any, is you with all your good intentions.

The Good News is:

The devil is God in disguise. He is all-inclusive. He is you. You are him. Don't believe it. Find out for yourself. Take your time (it usually takes many lifetimes). The Journey is part of the game. If it leads No-where, it is because you never left Home, really. You only thought you did (and many are eager to tell you that you've failed). In time you'll wake up.

Zen saying

"When there is attachment to a belief system, there is the need to defend it. The Buddha himself refused to engage in the debates about religious dogma that were popular in his time. He said at one point, "It is not I who argues with the world, but the world that argues with me." In the richness of his realization and compassion, he actually exhorted his followers to let go of all entangling identifications, including the burden of identifying with one's own path. He described his own teachings as a raft we use to traverse the river of suffering until we arrive at the other shore of peace. Once we have arrived there, we just let go of the raft. We do not continue to carry it around with us. Rigid identification with a system of beliefs arises in part from uncertainty and fear. When we don't feel connected to a personal sense of the truth, we become uneasy and cling to narrow views. If we feel deluded or confused we become frightened and look for something to hold on to, some kind of security somewhere. This is the picture of dogmatism, fanaticism, and conceit. The spiritual righteousness born from sectarian views provokes an immense feeling of separateness, of "us" and "them," of "being better than," which in the end proves to be a self-constructed prison, a highly decorated cage. By clinging to spiritual views in such a way, we use the mystery and beauty of spirituality as an object of exploitation, rather than as the key to immeasurable love." (Sharon Salzberg: A Heart as wide as the World) [114]

12. ACHIEVEMENT

Most people pursue "Happiness" in one way or another, whether envisaged as material and social success, or as well-being and joy. Usually there lurks a feeling of dissatisfaction, or even depression behind the seemingly good enterprise of hunting for a better life. Improvement and development are values seldom questioned. But there is a fundamental trap in this search for a better life: the harder you look, the more disappointed you will become. The striving steals your attention away from the reason for your dissatisfaction and still further from the NOW and HERE of the present moment, the only place and time where contentment and joy can be experienced. Most of the time we are lost in a dream of beliefs that cloud our perception and limit our appreciation of the joy of being.

Zen saying

"Because we are sunk in the delusion of ego-clinging, we think in terms of 'my body, my mind, my name'. We think we own them and take care of them. Anything that does them harm, we will attack. Anything that helps them, we will become attached to. All the calamities and loss that come from this are therefore said to be the work of ego-clinging and since this is the source of suffering, we can see that it is indeed our enemy. Our minds which cling to the illusion of self, have brought forth misery in samsara from beginning-less time. How does this come about? When we come across someone richer, more learned or with a better situation than ourselves, we think that they are showing off, and we are determined to do better. We are jealous, and want to cut them down to size. When those less fortunate than ourselves ask for help, we think, 'What's the point of helping a beggar like this? He will never be able to repay me. I just can't be bothered with him.' When we come across someone of equal status who has some wealth, we also want some. If they have fame we also want to be famous. If they have a good situation, we want a good situation too. We always want to compete. This is why we are not free from samsara: it is this that creates the sufferings and harm which we imagine to be inflicted on us by spirits and other human beings." (Dilgo Khyentse: Enlightened Courage) [82]

13. SOMETHING WRONG

Humanism is the stage of good intentions, concern about right and wrong, trying to be tolerant, trying to follow moral standards. However, there are lots of disappointments because it does not work very well. Gradually the hidden agenda behind good intentions surfaces. You suspect something is wrong. If you are good, someone else is bad. In a fundamental sense, saints create sinners.

At the next stage, that of Self Development, the focus is on self reflection, and self improvement. Here you recognise that good deeds require a genuine, caring, unselfish personality. Improve yourself, and others will benefit. Moreover, there is an increasing understanding of common destiny, sharing of problems, sharing of experience and awareness. There is less me/you, we/them, and more one-ness and similarity. We become more self-less, others and external events seem more selfless, more like ourselves. That's because they *are* ourselves (!).We only did not recognise it before now.

Zen saying

"You and I have, intrinsically, the capacity to see, hear, feel, and understand each other, as well as ourselves, clearly, directly, and wholly from instant to instant. We have the immediate capacity to be attentive, honest, undefended, intimate, and compassionate with each other, as well as with all other living things, not at some future date, but right now. We have the capacity to drop entirely the distracting, distorting, confusing limitations of a soap opera version of our lives that dominates our thinking most of the time. We have the ability to respond freely and effortlessly with love, affection, and understanding to each other and our environment this very moment. It is a fact that we have these possibilities, yet we do not seem to live this way. Why is this so? That most of us understand the importance of living with more awareness, wisdom, and love is a given. However, the nuts and bolts, exactly how to go about that on an everyday reallife basis often seem elusive, if not impossible. If we look carefully and honestly at the moment-to-moment reality of how we do live our lives, it seems apparent that we're not really here for the most part of it. We are oblivious so much of the time to the people, places, and things going on around us, almost as if we're half asleep, in a dream state of worries, regrets, longings, hesitations, and distractions. Indeed, it's probably not unfair to say that most of what we do, we do half-heartedly, as if we're not really sure we want to be here. The numbing effect this has on the quality of our lives is both undeniable and tragic." (Scott Morrison: Open and Innocent) [101]

14. BELIEF, HOPE, DOUBT

Belief and Doubt go together. Both are symptoms of clinging, of dependence on something "more" and "other" than oneself or the immediate world around us. There may be some stages or progress in the development or liberation from the need of having to believe in something:

a) The firm Believers: I am responsible or I should be in charge, have control of myself and my doings. When I fail, another One should be in charge and correct me. Especially, He should correct other people's wrongdoing. His will overrules mine (and especially the others!).

b) The Non-Believers: I am determined by my history and the current surroundings. But my free will overrule if I am sufficiently determined. I am either being influenced (= passive) or influencing (= active).

c) The Liberated: Who am I? Who is looking? Who is asking? Who is doing? Who is being pushed around ? Everything is Happening, but I am It. Everything is happening to me, including my own doings.

You are offered all kinds of "systems": political, religious, therapeutic, self developmental.

Are you looking for the Right system, guidance, solution? Have you ever asked yourself WHY do you want such a system? Why do you think you need it? It may be a deception, a beating around the bush, a deviation from seeing the heart of the matter, a pretence that you do not already know the answers your self? What if there *are* only wrong systems, in the sense that all prescriptions are deviation from the path of seeing for yourself, honestly observing what is, attentively responding to what is really happening in every moment?

Beware that this is a big issue. Believing in some form of system is at the very core of our culture and possibly also in your personality. However, it never hurts to look for yourself, ask questions, do not take anything for granted. Any decent system or institution should welcome wondering, criticism or alternative opinions. But be careful, intolerance or "besserwissen" is the rule, not the exception. Moreover, why was the organisation founded in the first place, if not to build boundaries between "us" and "others"?

(The obvious positive aspects of organising and organisations are well-known and therefore left out here. Awareness encompasses all aspects together).

Zen saying

"Who are you?

Ask yourself the following questions:

- What kind of a person do you believe yourself to be?
- Are you good-looking, ugly, or somewhere in the middle?
- Are you too skinny, too fat, or just right?
- Are you smart, dumb, or average?
- Are you a very hard worker, or do you think of yourself as generally unfocused?
- Are you capable of great things, or pretty average in your potential?
- Is life unfair or good to you?
- Are you receiving all that you deserve from life?
- Are people in your life generally trustworthy?
- Do you "fit in" when in social situations or are you an outsider?

Now take a moment and consider this: Any answer you gave was a belief. It was based solely on your perception of yourself and on your drama.

How might your beliefs limit you?

If any of those beliefs were to change, how could that improve your life?

What would it take to begin to let go of those beliefs?"

(Shannon Duncan: Present Moment Awareness)[35]

15. RIGHT/WRONG

Whatever you do, do not moralise to others, and do not try to improve yourself!

Just observe, the more accepting or detached, the better. The point is insight, preferably in here-and-now situations. The criterion for doing it "right", is when things get easier, nicer, less worrying, rather than more difficult, more full of conflict, more "challenging"!

However, your sensibility and keen observation also increase and introduce new tasks that you did not recognise previously. (This may be somewhat discouraging in terms of frustration, but is a part of the progress.) Again, the solution is to de-worry, de-dramatise, and simplify the situation. Use your frustrations as signals for situations which have the potential for being perceived as easier and consequently have the potential for better insight (and relaxation).

Zen saying

"However, realizing that holy and evil are but ideas in our minds doesn't turn us into terrorists. Quite the contrary: most terrorists seem to act from a strong sense of 'working towards a better world' by fighting the evil forces they believe are around. The fundamentalists of each religion have their own standards, and at some point they will encounter the fundamentalists of another belief. Each group believes that they are the good guys and the others the bad guys. Both of them have a strong sense that the others (the bad guys) must be punished or killed. Since each group has its own moral codes and its own sense of what is evil, and both groups believe their system is the best one, they will both do all they can to protect their own interests. Although we can all sense that there is indeed no good without bad because we fabricate them in the mind, we still seem to feel the need to stimulate or reward the ones we believe are good and fight or punish the ones we believe are bad. But does it really work that way? Can we influence the balance of right and wrong? Can we put light on the front of an object without creating a shadow on the back? What if good and bad are always balanced by each other, just like north pole and south pole? What if holy and evil are always compensating each other, just like left and right? If that were true, all our attempts to work for a better world would become useless. It is not easy to prove this, but if one compensated for the other it would be ridiculous even to try and manipulate the world. Trying to work towards Utopia is like wanting to have a landscape with more mountains, but *not* with more valleys. Maybe we would find out it is just like moving the furniture around. Trying to turn the universe into a better place is like hoping for a battery with only a positive pole. And this is also true for the spiritual quest: can we really work on a better future? There are always two sides to a coin. Maybe the back of the coin will also grow while we are working on the front."

(Jan Kersschot: This Is It)[81]

16. ETHICS

Concern about moral and ethics belong to a certain level of understanding. In Zen Psychology there are 4-5 levels or degrees of development of consciousness.

1. The first one may be termed "Dualism". There is a great deal of antagonism and separateness, loneliness here. The good is pitted against "the bad", "the bad ones" or "the others".

2. The next stage is termed "Humanism", the striving for common values, community, sharing, trying to be good, trying to do the right things. Fighting for cause and purpose, preferably not against people. However, the insight and identification with others are only partial. When stressed, you become provoked and fight, usually generating even

more confrontation in a vicious circle, much like the level 1 of Dualism.

3. At the next level of understanding, ("Self development"), there is a logical, conscious, apprehension (and appreciation) of our common nature, origin and well-being. Here you may become interested in Zen-literature or teachings. Not to mention thousands of other "alternative" spiritual, physical or therapeutic ways. The common inspiration is self improvement, development, perhaps combined with dissatisfaction with oneself, others or life. After a while – or after a very long time – one may see through this often frantic strive for perfection, see that it is in fact quite egoistic and ambitious, thus being counter-productive if you really want self improvement. An orientation towards being more self-less, less egoistic, may then appear and flourish, leading to the next level.

4. At this stage ("Seeking") you may now and then experience "one-ness" with the physical world, with others and with yourself. One starts to reveal the Ego and relaxes with regard to saving the world, others and notably oneself. But you are still a Seeker, not a Finder. Yet.

5. Finally ("Liberation") one may turn into a Finder or rather, "It" finds you, because you can not arrive at will, deliberately. The Ego can only try, and the harder it tries, the more hardened it (you) becomes, pinning you to the lower levels. But don't despair, all the levels are worth while for their own sake. Really. The more patient you are, the sooner you will arrive...

The levels in a nutshell may look like this:

1. Dualism = improving the world, physically

2. Humanism = improving the world, persons

3. Self development = improving oneself

4. Seeking = accepting oneself and the world

5. Liberation = living the world.

Zen saying

"Now the recovery of our extensive and inclusive type of awareness is completely different from the acquisition of a moral virtue, to be urged upon society by persuasion and propaganda and cultivated by discipline and practice. As we know, such idealisms are notorious for their failure. Furthermore, moral and spiritual idealisms with all their efforts and disciplines aimed at the future are forms of the very mode of awareness which is giving us the trouble. For they perceive good and bad, ideal and real, separatively and fail to see that "goodness" is necessarily a "bad" man's ideal, that courage is the goal of cowards, and that peace is sought only by the disturbed."
(Alan W. Watts: Nature, Man and Woman) [136]

17. LIFE QUALITY

For many people today there is a gradual shift of focus from Results and achievements to Process and being. The way of living, of well-being, becomes more important than success. Unfortunately, many people are too busy or entangled with their career or simply, job requirements, to have time for reflection, time for what really matters to them or time for change. In short, time-out. To find or regain oneself, the basic feeling of being, of oneness with nature, back to your senses – out of your mind! It is a pity if you wait until you retire or fall ill. Too many people go through a life full of obligations (real or imagined), and exit without having ever felt they lived to their potential or genuine interests.

Zen saying

"Take just a moment, if you will, to examine your life, not your life as thought about, but your life as you are actually living it right now. Be as honest with yourself as you can, and look carefully at all aspects: your relationships, your professional and financial behaviour, your social, religious, and political thoughts, opinions, and activities, your deepest and truest feelings about your body, your thoughts and emotional life, what you think of as "yourself," and other people. Are you at peace? Are you fully attentive in whatever you are doing? Do you love easily, freely, and without conditions? These are the elements of a happy life, a life worth living. This present moment is all that you have. It's all that you will ever have. So these questions are about how things are now. How you are living now is how you are living your whole life. Telling yourself things will be different at some future date is simply wishful thinking. Peace, joy, and creative happiness are a present possibility. It all depends on what you really want. To find out if this is true, you must let go of the grossly incomplete and inaccurate mental versions and ideas about your life that normally dominate your consciousness, and in so doing, allow yourself to be unguardedly and unconditionally curious about everyone and everything. Affection, compassion, and happiness are the natural results of that genuine curiosity. Can you do that? Most of us have already tested the alternatives, and come up way short. So, again, the fundamental question: Do you really want to be happy and at peace? It's a question of willingness: Just how much attention, openness, understanding, and kindness are you capable of, right here, right now?" (Scott Morrison: Open and Innocent) [101]

18. NEUROSIS

Neurosis is denial or displacement used as a protection against problems which are too unpleasant or incapable of being solved at that stage of development. It is an avoidance mechanism necessary at that time but limiting the behaviour later on. You are thus punished two times, first being forced into the neurosis, then later for having the neurosis, or "inadequate behaviour". The consequence is a double bind; you are damned if you do and damned if you don't, caught in a "Catch 22".

Neurosis may be seen as a kind of self-hate (punishing or restricting yourself on behalf of earlier persons of authority such as parents). Therein also lies a great opportunity. The "cause" of the neurosis lies in the past, it no longer really exists. You are now responsible (in an active sense, not a moral sense) for the punishment. And you are performing it now. However, it seems that you cannot help yourself, it *seems* like you do not want to have the problem. That is a very clever form of self-hate! If you are lucky to get a glimpse of yourself while wanting to have the problem, it disappears, vanishes. We can fool ourselves indefinitely, but not consciously – after the cat is out of the bag.

Zen saying

"We have no control but we think we *should* have.

Letting go of the illusion of control will not make you more vulnerable, it will make you more open, calm, joyful, relaxed, peaceful, and receptive.

Children have no control and don't think they should have. "Yes, but look what happens to kids!"

Life is life with or without the illusion of control. Children feel the pain of life, of course. But, pain and suffering is not the same thing. Suffering happens when we are taught to believe that what is happening to us is wrong and a mistake, and we should have prevented it!"

(Cheri Huber: There Is Nothing Wrong With You for TEENS) [74]

19. FRUSTRATION

Existential frustration is both a sign of maturity and of unfulfilled development. There is a progress from the most physical, materialistic conflicts to the light, spiritual awareness of happenings around you. From polarity between opposing views (and actions!) to acceptance of whatever happens. In between there are a variety of different kinds of frustration, which is the result of the negative feedback you receive from not being in harmony with yourself. Frustration is an opportunity for learning. It means you are close to being aware of what could have been handled in an easier way!

Which are the stages of this gradual development?

1. At first, there is a complete polarisation. The dangerous, the evil or hostile environment – physical world as well as people – is out there. This is paranoia. I, as an ego, must protect myself, fight against the external threats, against the world. Symptoms are suspicion, fear, aggression, violence, polarity, right and wrong absolutes. (Fundamentalism).

2. Next in evolution is an acknowledgement of good and evil characteristics also in oneself. An internal conflict, a battle between good and evil, responsibility, temptations, consciousness, morality.

3. Gradually we grow the insight and appreciation that this internal conflict is artificial and false. There is also a desire for harmony. We start seeking. There is confusion, self contradicting trials and errors. We discover the ego to be

egoistic, self-centred, pitiful, mean and frightful. We adopt all kinds of spiritual methods, gurus, traditions, therapies, myths, teachings. All propose eagerly to save your wretched soul – only you do your part by believing in or paying them. If it doesn't work, try harder...

4. Finally if and when the time is ripe, there will be an understanding that the ego cannot get rid of the ego (!). The ambition of eliminating the ego is just still another trick of the ego, strengthening itself as usual. At this point you are stuck with the paradox. Meeting the wall. Wants to stop Doing (using effort), but cannot practice no-doing, because that would be deliberate passivity, which definitely is also a kind of Doing (acting, willing, wanting, striving).

Laissez-faire is no solution; it is also a kind of deliberate passivity. Unfortunately, the solution cannot be told, not even be found. It may find you, however, if you are lucky some day. The mystics give us some hints:

No Resistance. Grace. Discovering oneself wanting to have the problems. Not making the problems, not asking.

Maybe the problem (and the solution) is artificial or virtual – doesn't really exist? Maybe the Question is the Answer? Maybe there never was an ego, even less so now? Who is asking then? Maybe there is no you, no personality, just the world and happenings? If there is no you, the world enters (or you enter). The World is You and You are the World. Why use two words for the same thing? Who are YOU? WHO is asking? YOU or ME? If none of this makes sense so far, please be assured you are not alone and you are in good company!

Zen saying

"This does not mean that you have to hide your anger. You have to let the other person know that you are angry and that you suffer. This is very important. When you get angry with someone, please don't pretend that you are not angry. Don't pretend that you don't suffer. If the other person is dear to you, then you have to confess that you are angry, and that you suffer. Tell him or her in a calm way. In true love, there is no pride. You cannot pretend that you don't suffer. You cannot pretend that you are not angry. This kind of denial is based on pride. "Angry? Me? Why should I be angry? I'm okay." But, in fact, you are not okay. You are in hell. Anger is burning you up, and you must tell your partner, your son, your daughter. Our tendency is to say, "I don't need you to be happy! I can be on my own". This is a betrayal of our initial vow to share everything. In the beginning you told each other, "I cannot live without you. My happiness depends on you." You made declarations like that. But when you are angry, you say the opposite: "I don't need you! Don't come near me! Don't touch me! "You prefer to go into your room and lock the door. You try your best to demonstrate that you don't need the other person. This is a very human, very ordinary tendency. But this is not wisdom. Happiness is not an individual matter. If one of you is not happy, it will be impossible for the other person to be happy."

(Thich Nhat Hanh: Anger) [49]

20. VIRTUAL REALITY

First of all, there is no Zen message! No theory, no methods, no obligations. At best there are suggestions and pointers, proposing and encouraging listeners to find out for themselves, to observe, to test, to experience.

When Zen is explicit, it is only as contrast to, as neutralisation of, theories (including common sense) claiming to describe reality with words.

The Reality pointed to in Zen is a non-verbal, directly perceived one. It cannot be described or presented or explained, nevertheless it is shared as direct experience of What Is.

Words, concepts, thoughts, all belong to the virtual world of imagination. This "Virtuality" is useful and thrilling when treated as such. "Virtuality" is dangerous and inhibiting if mistaken as reality. Everything we believe in or take for granted in common sense concepts is virtual in the sense of being products of the imagination, at best shadows of real events. We are all too willing to live in the shadows, fooling ourselves from being and doing what we really want and are meant to realise.

Zen saying

"Life's work is to wake up, to let the things that enter into the circle wake you up rather than put you to sleep. The only way to do this is to open, be curious, and develop some sense of sympathy for everything that comes along, to get to know its nature and let it teach you what it will. It's going to stick around until you learn your lesson, at any rate. You can leave your marriage, you can quit your job, you can go only where people are going to praise you, you can manipulate your world until you're blue in the face to try to make it always smooth, but the same old demons will always come up until finally you have learned your lesson, the lesson they came to teach you. Then those same demons will appear as friendly, warm-hearted companions on the path." (Pema Chödrön: The Places That Scare You) [27]

21. HAPPINESS

"Conditioning" is here the technical term for the formation of bad habits. Conditioning is therefore responsible for a certain delay or resistance after insight into our nature should have resulted in new behaviour and well-being.

The general feeling of sadness results from negative thoughts, which is a primary example of bad habits. The universal quest for Happiness is a reflection of this state of sadness, or un-happiness. Instead of the natural state of contentment and well-being, the sadness produces a desire for Happiness which only adds to the already long list of shortcomings. As a sign or symbol that "things could have been otherwise" however, the quest for Happiness may be useful motivation on the path of seeking and finding the way Home.

Zen saying

"Am I saying, "Enjoy this moment. Be happy"? No. Allow the "such-ness" of this moment. That's enough. Surrender is surrender to *this moment*, not to a story through which you *interpret* this moment and then try to resign yourself to it. For instance, you may have a disability and can't walk anymore. The condition is as it is. Perhaps your mind is now creating a story that says, "This is what my life has come to. I have ended up in a wheelchair. Life has treated me harshly and unfairly. I don't deserve this." Can you accept the *is-ness* of this moment and not confuse it with a story the mind has created around it? Surrender comes when you no longer ask, "Why is this happening to me?" " (Eckhart Tolle: Stillness Speaks) [128]

22. NOTHING WRONG WITH YOU

Zen may be quite contrary to the common sense beliefs, especially with respect to matters of moral conduct, responsibility and effort, the ego activities.

Conscience, for instance, is not always to be trusted. Good conscience, as when explicit, declared, imagined, may well be an excuse for performing dubious actions (or not taking actions). Look closely, at yourself and others whenever "good conscience" is expressed.

Likewise, bad conscience is a symptom of a person in conflict with himself. But who is in conflict with whom? Someone is fooling himself and probably others as well. Just observe, and see what the case is. Good conscience or rather, no worrying, no inner conflict, no self-hate, is the natural state of mind. Caring for others or changing our behaviour will arise when appropriate and rather not because of obligations or feeling of guilt or conflicting motives.

Therapy comes in all forms and may be appropriate according to the degree of stress and circumstances, an issue not to be treated uniformly. *If* you have a relaxed attitude to therapy however, this may be for you:

The Bad News is: There is nothing you can do about it… All you do to improve, will only increase the confusion and stress.

The Good News is: You do not need to do anything, since the problems are virtual. It has been OK all the time, right from the beginning. So, what's the Problem?

Acceptance of circumstances is a good start. Acceptance of others is good progress. Acceptance of yourself is the goal. Then everything has already changed (!).

Zen saying

"You were taught to believe that there is something wrong with you and that you are inadequate, but there isn't and you're not. Even if you grew up in a loving family, you learned to criticize and reject yourself to one degree or another. And, because you are intelligent, you learned to do it to yourself before anyone else could. It seems like it doesn't hurt quite so much that way. It you are not the person you want to be, it's probably not because you don't punish yourself enough. The more likely cause is that you don't love yourself enough. You are perfectly you, and you are all-potential." (Cheri Huber: There Is Nothing Wrong With You for TEENS) [74]

SELF DEVELOPMENT CHALLENGES

23. SELF DEVELOPMENT

The felt need for Self development implies that there is something wrong with you. And secondly, that you are able to correct it yourself.

Have you ever asked yourself if the perception of personal faults may in fact be wrong? For instance, the desire for improvement may reflect distrust and rejection of how you are and thus be the main problem itself. What if your shortcomings are misinterpretations, illusions? Or manufactured beliefs. There is nothing wrong with you. You only think so. And even that is not your fault or under your control. It only reflects your state of consciousness which is directed towards self-improvement and trying to regain control of your life. Which would be all right, if that was part of your nature. But it isn't. However, all this striving for improvement and excellence, although futile, is worthwhile, necessary and takes time – usually a very long time. It is part of our natural development. It may be interesting, heroic and frustrating. But some day it is time for going beyond this. Gradually the motivation will shift from improvement to acceptance, along with the surprising discovery that things go better the less you try (strive). Maturation grows through self-acceptance (and acceptance of others), not through self-hate, moralising, denial or struggling. Be aware that self-hate may well be disguised as trying to achieve "improvement" or development.

Zen saying

"In effect this dialogue acts as a mirror to one's own mind, because the teacher always throws back to the student the question he's asked! He really does not answer any questions at all, he merely tosses them back at you, so that you yourself will ask *why* you are asking it, and why you are creating the problem the question expresses. And quickly it becomes apparent that it is up to you. "Who, *me?*" you may ask. Yes, *you!* "Well," you may say, *"I* can't solve this problem. I don't know how to do it." But what do you mean by *you?* Who are you, really? Show me the you that cannot answer the question. It is in this kind of back-and-forth dialogue that you begin to understand. Through relationship with the other person you discover that it is you who's mixed up, and that you are asking the wrong questions! In fact, you are trying to solve the wrong problem altogether." (Alan Watts: What is Zen?) [153]

24. CONCEPTS

In modern culture, we believe that everything may be described in words and presented as methods and systems. All major conflicts are expressed through or with reference to verbal disagreements. It is as if the verbal symbols had an existence of their own and were not merely symbolic representations, pointing perhaps to non-existent events. The symbols signify by nature a virtual reality, which may or may not correspond with the actual world. More and more we mistake this virtual reality for the real one, distancing ourselves from observation of actual events and behaviour. Everything is "interpreted" and abstracted, defined, re-defined, filtered and theorised. Everything can be explained away or misunderstood. (Are you a terrorist or an idealist? Are you an aggressor or defender? Are you one of Us or the Other? Are you Good or Evil?).

The entertainment multimedia are rapidly growing more realistic, making it increasingly more difficult to distinguish between the virtual and the real, fact or fiction. This both intrigues us and frightens us, willingly. What should frighten us however, is the unconscious (unknown or disguised) virtuality of the everyday world of personal and political conflicts. The degree of technical virtuality is increasing, probably because it is a progress beyond the current understanding of human nature. The development of deliberate technical and experiential virtuality is so strong and fast that it may well signify the dawning of a new stage in human consciousness. It would be nice if this fascination with, and mastering of, deliberate virtuality, would eventually trigger a similar awareness of unconscious (unwanted, un-willed) virtuality. We certainly need a re-defining or re-finding of human nature and a return to a lost Paradise.

Zen saying

"Isn't everything you're talking about a concept?

Of course! The only truth which is not a concept is the sense of presence, here and now. In the impersonal sense of presence, "I Am," not "I am Joe or Jane." This impersonal sense of presence in the present moment is the only truth.

Whether it is Maharshi's approach, or Maharaj's or yours, it is a concept.

Oh yes, but both of them made it perfectly clear: nothing has been created, nothing has been destroyed. It's all a dream, and there is no individual, other than an appearance in Consciousness.

Does awakening lead to awareness which persists twenty-four hours a day?

Yes, but there is no one to be conscious of that awareness. That is the key to the whole thing. There is no individual, no ego

to be conscious of that awareness. Awareness is just there!"
(Ramesh S. Balsekar: Consciousness Speaks) 8

25. MEDITATION

How may we turn worrying thoughts into useful tools?

1. It is important to know that thoughts are not significant in themselves. They are not dangerous, not difficult and do not represent real problems.

2. Thoughts only have power to the extent they are believed in. Otherwise, they are shadows, illusions, superstition, and nightmare. This is really important to know and understand.

3. Thoughts will always protect the ego, and therefore seem to be friendly. Beware, they may well represent self-hate, and then in the next moment blame yourself for hating yourself.

4. Observation (introspection) of thoughts (and feelings) is extremely useful for discovering the virtual nature of thoughts.

5. At some stage during meditation, the thoughts will calm down and fade away. This stillness is vital. It cannot be over-estimated. It is your core of basic awareness, consciousness, and your ground of being. It is usually clouded by all your worries and inner chatter, preventing full attention and perception of the moment, preventing you from being fully in the here and now, preventing spontaneity and joy. In time, you will grow a willingness to be "thought-less" (!) and to be present un-conditionally, free from future and past.

6. Use thoughts and meditation systematically (every day or week or month) as opportunities for liberation: observation, awareness, insight, practice, testing. Your exercise does not have to be done while sitting formally. Self-awareness may

well be practised while driving, waiting in meetings, etc. There are also abundant good prescriptions for more formal meditation, if you have the opportunity and inclination for that.

Zen saying

"The experience of labelling your thoughts "thinking" also, over time, becomes much more vivid. You may be completely caught up in a fantasy, in remembering the past or planning for the future, completely caught up, as if you had gotten on an airplane and flown away someplace. You're elsewhere and you are with other people and you've redecorated a room or you've relived a pleasant or unpleasant experience or you've gotten all caught up in worrying about something that might happen or you're getting a lot of pleasure from thinking about something that may happen, but you're completely involved as if in a dream. Then suddenly you realize, and you just come back. It happens automatically. You say to yourself, "Thinking," and as you're saying that, basically what you are doing is letting go of those thoughts. You don't repress the thoughts. You acknowledge them as "thinking" very clearly and kindly, but then you let them go. Once you begin to get the hang of this, it's incredibly powerful that you could be completely obsessed with hope and fear and all kinds of other thoughts and you could realize what you've been doing, without criticizing it, and you could let it go. This is probably one of the most amazing tools that you could be given, the ability to just let things go, not to be caught in the grip of your own angry thoughts or passionate thoughts or worried thoughts or depressed thoughts." (Pema Chödrön: The Places That Scare You) [27]

26. SEEKING

Everyone wants Happiness for oneself and those we care for. Some people are more dedicated, conscious or systematic in how they go about this. They are not necessarily more successful in their endeavour. There is a catch in the very act of seeking. If the challenge is being in the Moment, Now, then seeking is a detour, a postponement. Even being a doer, making effort, desiring Happiness, is an obstacle, and is *the* obstacle. NO RESISTANCE to what Is and what Happens, may be a very good suggestion. Experiment with it, test it out! Some wise men speak about Grace, the divine reception without achievement. A first step is to start questioning the truth of the many obligations and admonitions. Then test them in your daily life by simply observing what happens. There are signs everywhere anytime for those who are willing to see. Seeing is changing. For instance, when you see (experience) that you really want to "fail" (be nervous, be depressed, criticize yourself, or whatever), the problem dissolves because you stop fooling yourself, pretending to be helpless. Experiment with this! It is exciting, dare yourself. The "Problem" may turn out to be virtual. It "only" looked real (which may be bad enough).

Zen saying

"The ego wants a target to aim at, a goal to work for, a special path to walk, and will never accept that there is nowhere to go to find Beingness, that there is no path to follow to become enlightened. The mind will try to tell us that it will take us to enlightenment through a process, by working it out. Liberation has nothing to do with hope and effort but with being childlike and being in wonder at what is. Still, the professional seeker prefers a path, a goal. One may even come with a technique to become more childlike, or try to be more flexible, try to accept everything as it is. One of the most popular goals in the spiritual path is trying to live in the 'here and now', and the problem appears when this is interpreted as a new task, when 'living in the here and now' is presented as a new personal goal. Where is this person who is supposed to be 'in the here and now'? How can we *not* be here? How can we *not* be in the now? Even when we think about our holiday in France last summer, our thoughts are still here and now. Here and now often suggests the existence of a 'there and then' which refers to a process in space and time. All of these concepts are toys of the mind, the Light doesn't care or even know about these." (Jan Kersschot: This Is It) [81]

27. EGO

Descartes said: "I think, therefore I am". In Zen I say: "I think, therefore I am not". There is no thinker, only thoughts. There is no thinker existing as separate from the thoughts or feelings. Look for yourself, test it. Malapropos, "looking for your self" is a futility if there is no you, no ego. Trying to "find yourself" is an impossible task, not because it is difficult, but because it is meaningless. Compare this viewpoint with psychology and all other systems for self-understanding. It is contrary to almost all accepted forms of self improvement. It is contrary to common sense.

Trying to find oneself is not only a virtual problem, it is The problem. The question (seeking, missing) is the problem itself. Therefore the Answer resides in the Question.

Thoughts are by their nature *virtual*, in the sense that they are only symbolic representations, whether of "real" events or of hypothetical events. Almost all our problems are thoughts, usually in the form of worries masquerading as real threats while in fact being virtual.

Zen saying

"Where does the ego come from?

The ego comes from only one place, from the only thing that exists all the time and that is Consciousness. That is why Ramana Maharshi says, "Find out the source of the ego.

Who is doing this? Who wants to know?" The mind cannot find an answer. The point of this questioning is not to find an answer. But when there is no answer, the mind settles down. The ego is not something to be ashamed of or frightened of. The ego is merely a reflection of that same impersonal Consciousness. This understanding takes the ego back to its source. It is mainly being afraid of the ego that is the problem. Accept the ego, along with everything else, as part of the functioning of the Totality and merely watch what happens. Then there is no trouble.

How does one accept the ego?

The average person who is not a seeker is not worried about his ego. He's perfectly content to be the ego. The seeker has been told, conditioned for years and years, "The ego is the problem. You must kill the ego, you must do this, you must do that." So the seeker, in the very beginning, is told the ego is the bad guy. "You must get rid of him." Who is to get rid of him? The ego is not prepared to commit *hara-kiri.* It will resist. That is why, in moments of meditation or quiet, the ego is frightened and says, "Don't waste your time, this is ridiculous. Go about your business, *do* something."

Does the ego disappear completely when enlightenment comes?

Ego disappears completely after the enlightenment is complete, in the sense that the sense of personal doer-ship disappears. Then for all practical purposes, the ego has disappeared. The identification with the body continues because the body-mind has to function. The identification as the individual doer disappears." (Ramesh S. Balsekar: Consciousness Speaks) [8]

28. CONSCIOUSNESS/AWARENESS

Awareness or consciousness is the most precious thing we have. And yet, we misunderstand it fundamentally. Awareness is not only the little, conscious part represented by thoughts and images, choices, frustrations or deliberate acts. Awareness includes mostly the unconscious background, context and environment in totality. Even more basic, awareness and consciousness is this totality and does not exist apart from it. Seeing WHAT IS is therefore profoundly misunderstood if pictured just as *observing* some events in the external world. Seeing is a direct access to the reality of a world aware of itself. Interpretations, categorising, comparisons, evaluations, discriminations: these are all verbal add-ons with dubious validity.

Zen saying

"Is stillness just the absence of noise and content? No, it is intelligence itself, the underlying consciousness of which every form is born. And how could that be separate from who you are? The form that you think you are, came out of that and is being sustained by it. It is the essence of all galaxies and blades of grass; of all flowers, trees, birds, and all other forms. Stillness is the only thing in this world that has no form. But then, it is not really a thing, and it is not of this world. When you look at a tree or a human being in stillness, who is looking? Something deeper than the person. Consciousness is looking at its creation. In the Bible, it says that God created the world and saw that it was good. That is what you see when you look from stillness without thought." (Eckhart Tolle: Stillness Speaks) [128]

29. IMPROVEMENT

The ultimate form of self development or improvement is the quest for "Enlightenment": liberation, total freedom or bliss.

It is tempting to believe that Enlightenment may be achieved at will. Our wise men, women and mystics warn us. Mind cannot get rid of mind, ego cannot eliminate ego. Indeed, the very desire for Enlightenment is the main obstacle, or The obstacle against attaining it. We then have only two options:

1. To understand (fundamentally) that there is nothing we can do to attain it.

2. To will (accept) what we are, here and now, inclusive our insecurity, desires, shortcomings, imperfections, antagonistic reactions

This acceptance is not the same as pessimism or laissez-faire (which is deliberate unconcern towards others). Luckily, we do not have to choose between 1 and 2 because they are the same (!).

Zen saying

"NOTICING OR NEUTRALLY
OBSERVING YOUR LIFE
WITHOUT TRYING TO MANIPULATE
OR CHANGE WHAT YOU SEE
IS ACTUALLY THE ESSENCE OR
KEY COMPONENT OF TRANSFORMATION.
ANOTHER WORD FOR THIS
NON-JUDGMENTAL SEEING
IS AWARENESS."
(Ariel & Shya Kane: Working on Yourself Doesn't Work) [77]

30. ZEN COMMANDMENTS

What should we do? If external systems are not accountable, may we follow our internal evaluations, our conscience? Our bad conscience is not a good lead since it is based on self-hate and confusion. A person in conflict with oneself is not to be trusted. Is there an alternative? We may try to formulate the negative or balancing expressions of what are considered to be truths in common sense. Let us see what happens when we identify the Zen Commandments. I believe the radicalism of Zen will become quite visible. At the same time, how can we avoid being perceived as just offending? Perhaps it may help to remind us that also Zen (and its many precursors) is basically concerned about ethics, i.e. the right way of living. Being ethical in this context means to be true to oneself and the world. Trusting and being true. Integrity, sanity and being ethical are thus the same according to this perspective. If the Zen Commandments for some people thus may appear to be irresponsible or disrespectful, they are certainly not meant to be that way. They are however, suggesting an alternative perspective of what it really means to be ethical.

The Zen Commandments

1. **You shall not have any gods**.

   Everyone and everything is God in disguise, but avoid any form of idolatry: of yourself, of people, religion or political systems. Trust nature, trust yourself and trust others.

2. **There is nothing Wrong with you.**

   Good conscience – or rather, no worrying, no inner conflict, no self-hate – is the natural state of mind.

3. **You and others and nature are One.**

   Therefore we are also "equal", naturally friendly and not alien or dangerous.

4. **Stop Pretending to be helpless or unhappy.**

   Stop blaming the past, others or yourself.

5. Do not be concerned about Right or Wrong.

It breeds a distrust of yourself and a distrust of others.

6. Stop trying to Improve or save yourself, others or the world.

Help when opportunity arises, not as an obligation, nor in pride. There are lots of opportunities, every day.

7. Trust your senses, wisdom and Spontaneity.

Trust the moment, your spontaneity, see what happens, and see What Is. Watch out for your (and others) thinking, ideas, prescriptions. Especially the idealistic or moralistic ones.

8. Question even the most accepted or advocated "Truths" or obligations.

"Common sense" and "good intentions" may sometimes be the most untrue and damaging ones. See for yourself, look *who* is proclaiming. Beware if you or others want to gain something.

9. You don't need to Control everything.

Accept Reality, what is here and now, not the virtual world of concepts, improvements, self-improvement, free will, confrontation, ambition, responsibility, competition, winning and false modesty.

10. No Resistance – is Liberating.

When the time is right, you will stop the game of pretence. You wake up and start living to your potential and joy. Allow others the same and rejoice in their spontaneity and happiness. They certainly do not have to be like you, but sometimes you must also look after yourself.

Zen saying

"Do you carry feelings of guilt about something you did, or failed to do, in the past? This much is certain: you acted according to your level of consciousness or rather, unconsciousness at that time. If you had been more aware, more conscious, you would have acted differently. Guilt is another attempt by the ego to create an identity, a sense of self. To the ego, it doesn't matter whether that self is positive or negative. What you did or failed to do was a manifestation of unconsciousness, human unconsciousness. The ego, however, personalizes it and says, "I did that," and so you carry a mental image of yourself as "bad." Throughout history humans have inflicted countless violent, cruel, and hurtful acts on each other, and continue to do so. Are they all to be condemned; are they all guilty? Or are those acts simply expressions of unconsciousness, an evolutionary stage that we are now growing out of? *Jesus'* words, "Forgive them for they know not what they do," also apply to yourself." (Eckhart Tolle: Stillness Speaks) [128]

31. PRETENDING

If you are discontent with yourself, you have a great opportunity in store for you. But usually in a very different direction than you are looking now. Often in the opposite direction. Ask yourself: Why am I discontent? Who is being discontent with whom? Why do you split yourself into "I being discontent with Me"? Don't fool yourself. The way you are is the way you really want to be. If you honestly want to be otherwise, just be so. If it is outside of your capabilities or opportunities, then it is wishful thinking. That is no problem either, just leave it. Being discontent only means that you are fooling yourself, pretending to want something you can't be, or pretending to want something you don't want. You still prefer to be discontent? That's okay too – it's a popular game to play. You win as long as you lose!

You are not dependant on other participants, you can do it all by yourself. Self-hate is a clever game.

Zen saying

"Ultimately, the inability to choose how we will act in the face of our emotions lies in our attempt to avoid feeling them altogether. This is yet another disastrous consequence of clinging or aversion and, ultimately, our refusal to accept What Is. All emotions are an inevitable part of our existence that cannot and will not be denied. If we are feeling an emotion, then there is a reason for it. We can investigate whether or not that reason is based in reality, but what we cannot do is deny that emotion its natural existence. In being present in the moment and allowing emotions to pass through us, we not only reduce their demands on our bodies, but we also gain the opportunity to understand their origins." (Shannon Duncan: Present Moment Awareness) [35]

32. ACCEPTANCE

When things do not go your way time after time, that's frustrating. Take a step back, look at the situation from the outside. Include the frustration and hopeless situation as part of your task. The conflict disappears as a problem, it turns into a different task or situation which you will naturally deal with differently than before. What the actual solution will be is an open answer. By including the frustration, you have excluded your ego from the conflict, and transformed the situation from a problem to a task or just a happening. Furthermore, your ego involvement itself may well have been a big part of the problem in the first place!

The Bad News is that you really want to keep the problems — for now.

The Good News is: Accept yourself, completely, full-heartedly. Don't resist. Accept others as well, they are really a part of you.

Zen saying

"In learning to live in the present moment with my own reactive clinging and aversion, I was able to let go of many of my limiting beliefs and begin to tear down the drama I lived within. As I stayed present with my Negative Core Beliefs instead of hiding from them, I found that I had deeply relaxed. I now flowed through life instead of struggling with it. My compassion for other people, and most importantly myself, has deepened immeasurably as I have learned to appreciate my own value as a human being. In living in the present moment, I have learned that life will always have its ups and downs, its triumphs and tragedies, its good days and bad, but through it all, life is a joy to experience and a gift that I will never again take for granted. For me, living in the present moment has become easier as it has become a way of life. This shift in perspective has opened my eyes to the fact that every day offers new joys, lessons, and opportunities." (Shannon Duncan: Present Moment Awareness) [35]

33. NO THEORY

In Zen there is no prescription, no theory. This is said to be a characteristic of Man, Nature and the way things work or happens.

This has a lot of implications.

Firstly as a renunciation of everything one may believe in, inclusive of ethical norms, religious predicaments, political systems, culture, psychology – even what is regarded as common sense and taken for granted. Zen is of course not anti-theoretical, nor anti-scientific or anti-technological. The a-theoretical perspective relates to the nature of Man and appears antagonistic when *compared* to the over-intellectualised, over-verbalised, over-conscious, over-controlled society of today.

Since religion is typically represented by very strong, accentuated and usually controlling belief systems, Zen may rightly be seen as very radical but not necessarily controversial. There will be no verbal debates, because Zen does not believe (!) in theoretical controversies, nor does it advocate an alternative theory. Zen is not happy with advocating at all. Which should be no surprise since everything is regarded as natural and appropriate whatever the appearance may be.

Zen saying

"Let me tell you again one of the most beautiful stories ever devised, the story of Adam's fall. It says that God forbade Adam to eat from the Tree of Knowledge. Zen will agree perfectly, because it is knowledge that is making you stupid, it is knowledge that is not allowing you to know. Adam was capable of knowing before he ate the fruit from the Tree of Knowledge. The moment he ate knowledge, the moment he became knowledgeable, he knew no more. The innocence was lost; he became cunning and clever. That intelligence was lost. Yes, he started growing in intellect, but intelligence was no longer there. Intellect has nothing to do with intelligence; it is just the contrary, the opposite. The more you are an intellectual, the less intelligent you are bound to be. Intellect is a substitute to hide your unintelligence; it is counterfeit. You don't have intelligence so you substitute it with intellect. It is, of course, cheap. You can purchase it anywhere, it is available. In fact, people are too willing to impart their knowledge to you. They are ready to throw all their rubbish on you. Adam became knowledgeable; hence the fall. So knowledge is the fall." (Osho: Zen: The Path of Paradox) [106]

34. CONTROL ONESELF

To get more control of your life seems like an unquestionable goal. It may hide several *misunderstandings*. It presupposes *free will*, but why then did you lose control in the first place? It presupposes that you are able to pull yourself together, as if against yourself? It assigns *responsibility* to yourself and others for circumstances and dispositions which are given and not chosen. Even if you focus on the potential for improvement, you cannot avoid blaming those (yourself or others) who do not "perform to their fullest", or find themselves in less fortunate life situations. You cannot be accountable for making your own happiness without also accounting for your own unhappiness. This great intolerance towards the less lucky ones is strongly disguised, but has devastating consequences regarding the status, health politics, respect for others, condemnation of the weak, the sick, or those addicted to drugs or alcohol. We feel much more comfortable when we, often without saying so, can regard it smugly as their own fault. They only got what they deserved and we do not need to be *so* concerned about them. It is sufficient to pity them a little...?

In general, look out for these kinds of fundamental Misunderstandings:

control, improvement, moralising, free will, responsibility, guilt, condemnation, fear of unpleasant experiences. All this is part of our common sense and is taken for granted. Nevertheless, it is easy to see through the positive or negative appearance if one just dares to look for oneself.

Is there a common denominator for these misunderstandings? Our view of human nature is a good candidate. We define ourselves as *separate* from nature in general, as independent, strong, responsible egos with Personality and Consciousness confronting the environment perceived as the Other. This apparently minor, self evident and logical split between Me and the Other world is schizophrenic and the root of all insane divisions and conflicts. *If* the Ego is different from the World, then it has to defend itself whenever threatened or expand whenever the opportunity arises. If the Ego does not exist (apart from in our imagination), then there is no conflict, no Problem, and there never was. It is worth while to consider.

Zen saying

"The way of Zen is thus supremely practical. Although we all tie ourselves up in knots with our ideas and feelings, the way through generally begins with acting purposefully now. Know your purpose at this moment and there is no difficulty knowing what to do. Paradoxically, perhaps, being able to act this way means letting go of trying to control tomorrow or yesterday. Simply do the right thing now." (David Brazier: Zen therapy: transcending the sorrows of the human mind) [22]

35. PEACE OF MIND

For those who have matured somewhat beyond the materialistic, physical state of consciousness, the quest for Happiness also includes a desire for Peace of mind. That is when the seeking really takes off. From then on, any obstacle, problem, frustration, conflict may work as a koan, a "take-on" for the seeker trying to solve, trying to understand, trying to improve. Whenever we are lucky, the koan or personal problem turns into an obvious task, a virtuality or misunderstanding which reveals its artificial nature. Eventually, the Answer is found in the Asking, where it in fact had been all the time. That is the end of Asking and there is no need for Answers. That is peace of mind. Now open to the World. You have lost yourself but found a whole world. It is yours. No, it is You, you are It.

Zen saying

"The Peace That Depends on Nothing:

We do not create peace. Peace is the easiest, most natural, wide open, intimate, infinite context into which everything, all experiences, thoughts, feelings, sensations, perceptions, circumstances, and so on, are born. We become aware of peace when we stop neurotically fixating on dualistic and conflictive mental activity, that is, when we stop:

clinging, craving,
hoping, demanding,
expecting, worrying, fearing,
resenting, judging,
denying, avoiding, resisting,
attacking, condemning, blaming, hating,
competing, excluding, gossiping, lying,
disliking, complaining, whining,
indulging in guilt and self loathing,
hurting ourselves,
hurting others,
and holding onto how we want things to be.
When the motives behind these are at rest or
abandoned altogether, our awakened nature, which
is intimate and kind, is free to express itself in
everything.
That's peace."
(Scott Morrison: Open and Innocent) [101]

36. PSYCHOTHERAPY

Although still stigmatized as a taboo, psychotherapy has been gradually more accepted and widespread in modern societies. To some degree psychotherapy has also come to be seen as a way of personal development, not only treatment of illness or disorders of the mind. An evaluation of psychotherapy (in general, or different methods or traditions) is far beyond the scope of this commentary. However, there is at least one reason for concern about the kind of human nature advocated.

Psychotherapy usually presupposes that something is wrong with you, often with causes way back in childhood. These causes or situations must be identified, understood and perhaps re-experienced in the therapeutic situation. Then you can start working on yourself and change behaviour. (There are great variations around these themes, for instance techniques and theories with more or less focus on the need for "going back").

From a Zen point of view, these pillars of psychotherapy may be fundamentally wrong. *If* that being the case, the therapeutic approach may be a long detour, similar to all the other kinds of prescriptions for self development and improvement.

It is always comforting to believe in something, whether it is religion, therapy or political ideology. And the placebo effect should work for some time. And the justification by the followers (of any direction) provides for positive reporting of healing effects and the need for recruiting more followers.

Zen saying

"These days, at such times, we are apt to seek out a therapist to, if I may change the metaphor, help us get the dragon back into its cave. Therapists of many schools will oblige in this, and we will thus be returned to what Freud called 'ordinary unhappiness' and, temporarily, heave a sigh of relief, our repressions working smoothly once again. Zen, by contrast, offers dragon-riding lessons, for the few who are sufficiently intrepid. I have always been aware, therefore, that Zen is a therapy, if a rather unusual one, and in this book I present it as such. It tells what Zen in particular, and Buddhism in general, has to teach us about transcending the sorrows of the human mind. Shakyamuni discovered how human ill-being works and how such understanding offers a path to liberation. The path is Zen. Zen is simply the heart of all Buddhist practice. I will draw on sources from many branches of Buddhism, and, indeed, some from outside Buddhism. No one has a monopoly on truth. Who can say a word of truth? Can you say it now? Why not? Because we live lives conditioned by the past and future. This is examined in Buddhist psychology and I will therefore include a substantial section on that subject. I will also describe the essential characteristics of the path of the **bodhisattva,** the person who lives on the way to enlightenment, for the sake of all sentient beings. This is the Buddhist model of the ideal therapist. At the end of the book, I will look more at the application of this path to the sufferings of individuals and the world. I hope to convey the essential Zen message that everything that happens is a doorway to liberation. Spiritual enlightenment is always available, irrespective of what the past or future may hold. Zen is to be free of all that. Even in the midst of the ordinary world we can establish our lives on new ground." (David Brazier: Zen therapy: transcending the sorrows of the human mind) [22]

37. NO DOING

On the path of liberation, there are many things that are easy to understand. But many are also very hard to accept. The closer we get to the ego, the core of our personality, the harder it becomes. Free will, or our *doing* is at the very centre.

Ego, free will, me as a person, me as a doer, me as different from the environment, me as different from other people, will-power as different from what happens, me as responsible, others as responsible, thinking as different from thoughts, planning and intention as different from spontaneous actions and perception...

These are our dearest values and abilities. To let them go, you
– as a person (as a personal, self-conscious mind) – must be
willing to "die"…

Zen saying

"Love, as I see it, is compassion. And love is something you cannot
create. As I see it, love or compassion is something which arises
with the understanding. So when the sense of personal doer-ship
leaves, then love and compassion automatically arise. When
you understand that actions which take place through your own
body-mind organism are not your actions, and thus the actions
which take place through other body-mind organisms are not
their actions, whichever way they may seem to affect you, then
there is deep understanding that what exists in all organisms,
that which brings about all actions, is the same Consciousness.
Compassion prevails when there is no judging and condemning.
Understanding produces compassion or love, or charity,
whatever you choose to call it. You cannot ask that love be
created in you. You cannot turn toward God until the turning
away from the self has occurred. So the turning away from the
self occurs first and then the turning toward God or Reality or
whatever. That is why I keep saying it is a matter of Grace. So you
can say, when love or compassion arises, it is a matter of Grace."
(Ramesh S. Balsekar: Consciousness Speaks) [8]

SEEKING CHALLENGES

38. LIBERATION

The Bad News is that the Ego cannot get rid of itself.

The more it tries, the stronger it gets. Self improvement is a
typical ego-activity.

The Good News is that there is no need to eliminate the Ego, because it does not really exist, and never did! The Ego is a fiction, a virtual construct with no influence other than our belief in it. The illusion fades when the belief in it is weakened.

The Ego or Ego-illusion is one of the most central, currently destructive but potentially liberating dreams in our process of awakening. It is the core of our virtual reality.

Zen saying

"Expansion in love is an action that is available to every being in the universe all the time. A willing awareness will take us to heaven, a loving attitude will make us free. Nothing else controls our fate. Good or bad behaviour is secondary. Whatever you are doing, love yourself for doing it. Whatever you are thinking, love yourself for thinking it. Love is the only dimension that needs to be changed. If you are not sure how it feels to be loving, love yourself for not being sure of how it feels. There is nothing on earth more important than the love which conscious beings feel towards each other, whether or not it is ever expressed."

(Thaddeus Golas: The Lazy Man's Guide to Enlightenment) [44]

39. APPEARANCE

All you know about is *appearances*. How you have spent your life so far, how you are doing now, what you plan to do, what you think about others, are all appearances, whatever the Reality might be. We have no choice but to go on playing, along with other people, animals, trees, flowers, mountains and beyond. If our deeds are not our own doing, they are at least IT's doing, and we are IT as much as anything else. And the IT we know, so happens to be conscious of itself, Nature is looking at Itself. Wow. That's something!

Zen saying

"By now you should have an idea of how our beliefs can distort our view of reality for as long as we fail to question them. When our perception changes, our thoughts and behaviour cannot help but change accordingly. This type of shift in self-awareness is very powerful, because as we deepen our understanding of whom we actually are as opposed to who we believe and thus limit ourselves to be, we begin to manifest a life that we genuinely enjoy living." (Shannon Duncan: Present Moment Awareness) [35]

40. PARADOXES

The chameleon changes its colour with the surroundings. Which colour does she have in front of a mirror?!

This koan may be a metaphor for "Everything is relative, but what is real then?" Many situations are seemingly paradoxical – especially in a verbal world. Anyway, out of nothing, in spontaneity, with no causes, things happen, people act, situation changes, arises, the Nature looks at itself and is surprised!

Zen saying

"Enlightenment is the very process of expanding, not of arriving at a different set of limits. There is no one correct way of looking at life "after" enlightenment. We are not obliged to be or not be anything, as long as in our hearts and minds we are whole. What does it mean, to be whole? It means that we must be willing to conceive of, to contain within ourselves, whatever is "other than" any limited idea. It means knowing that when we emphasize a positive, we are at the same time creating a negative. When we choose an ideal of knowledge, then we must deal with the ignorance that is other than the knowledge. When we emphasize an ideal of holiness, then we must live with the sin that is its companion, and accept our responsibility for having created it. If we deny doing so, that is a contraction of awareness; we become dense, we become mass-level entities, we are incarnated in physical bodies. And we cannot control what we have denied creating, it is forced into our attention whether we like it or not, and so we live in a world of sin and ignorance. However, if we remain constantly open and unresisting to such negatives, we are not compelled to dwell on them; if we allow that ugliness is always within us, then we are free to create beauty. If we know that stupidity is always within us, then we are free to emphasize this intelligence. Love is the highest and holiest action because it always contains that which is not love within itself, it always and ever moves to include the unloving."

(Thaddeus Golas: The Lazy Man's Guide to Enlightenment) [44]

41. EXERCISES

When it has been recognised that one has to find the answers within oneself, then a new line of development with several stages in certain succession begins.

The problem is that one thinks that life is a problem which is supposed to be understood and solved. Then we shall be happy again and return to the bliss that many remember from their childhood.

1. The first step in the right direction is to get some – and a great deal of – experience with the fact that *problem solving* does not work.

2. Thereupon there is some realisation that the very attempt to solve the problems is the problem itself, or creates more problems.

3. Then the experience that Problems are the result of a Misunderstanding, an illusion, and that perhaps nothing is really wrong.

4. Furthermore, to understand what the Misunderstanding really is. This understanding is quite contrary to everything we thought was right and important. It even counters what we reckon as most important, precious and personal: identity, independent individual actions, ego, free will, responsibility, and good deeds.

   One thing is to hear about this and believe it to some degree. *That leads to a desire to eliminate the ego.* Later understanding reveals that this is not possible (because trying to get rid of the ego is just another ego activity). One sees the perils of the ego, wants strongly to eliminate it, and sees that it is not possible. This is a double bind. You are damned if you do, and damned if you don't.

5. Then what? That is the big question. What do you do when you cannot do anything? Gradually you will see that it is not necessary to do anything. You do not have to change, improve. Things and people are much more natural and good than you ever expected. Even more important is to see that you yourself are not bad. You are not only OK but great. We think we have been out of line. We certainly are frustrated about it. This seems to demonstrate the ultimate proof that something *is* wrong. Actually, the frustration only proves that you are in conflict and feel discomfort, which is both natural and representative of the way you are just now, which again is a natural stage in the development. The discomfort is Nature's way of giving feedback, and generally the conflicts are necessary intermediate experiences before further progress.

6. Finally, you recognise that these "faults" (of others, of yourself, of events, ego-striving, self-criticism) actually *are willed* or become willed through acceptance. Then,

paradoxically, the problem dissolves. Finally you are willingly (but not through free will!) in harmony with the natural way of things. Experiences (and actions as well) happen and are welcomed. They are no longer perceived as wrong or right, threatening, flattering, forced, personally accomplished or failed. Right/wrong or success/failure fades from the perception. In the end you and the world are one. You are the World, the world is You. In this world there are other people who no longer are "others" separate from yourself. The belonging, identification, constitutes an indisputable acceptance, that is the perception of and love of What is and that which is You.

Zen saying

""Well," you might say, "how can we stop? We think perpetually, we are always talking to ourselves. It's a nervous habit!" To stop thinking, there are certain technical aids: Concentrate on breathing, and think of nothing but your breathing, in and out, in and out.... One, two, three, four, five. One, two, three, four, five.

Or look at a point of light and think of nothing else but the point of light, just concentrate, concentrate, on that light. Both of these help you to eliminate all concepts from the mind except that which you are concentrating on. The next thing is to get rid of the point you're concentrating on. Most people think that means a "blank mind," but it doesn't. You concentrate on something in order to cause the thought process, the verbalizing, to stop. Then when you take away the point of concentration, you simply perceive the world *as it is,* without verbalizing." (Alan Watts: What is Zen?) [153]

42. SPONTANEITY

How to develop, attain or regain Spontaneity? Spontaneity is the natural state of mind. It will be "attained" when we remove the obstacles. These obstacles are "willed". They are imposed by ourselves although we have originally been trapped into doing so by criticism from others or self-criticism (which is only an internalisation of the original criticism). Spontaneity is the opposite of struggling, striving, planning, worrying, choosing, comparing, fearing, condemning, exerting free will and will-power.

Spontaneity takes care of itself if you just let go:

1. No Thinking

2. No Improvement

3. No Doing

4. No Resistance

The positive implications are:

a) It is not necessary to correct anything, not even The Misunderstanding (the illusion of separateness).

b) It is not possible to correct anything.

The combined effect of this insight of "no need" and "vain effort" provides for liberation. The greater the insight, the less frustration.

Zen saying

"On the surface it seems that the present moment is only one of many, many moments. Each day of your life appears to consist of thousands of moments where different things happen. Yet if you look more deeply, is there not only one moment, ever? Is life ever not "this moment"? This one moment, Now, is the only thing you can never escape from, the one constant factor in your life. No matter what happens, no matter how much your life changes, one thing is certain: it's always Now. Since there is no escape from the Now, why not welcome it, become friendly with it? When you make friends with the present moment, you feel at home no matter where you are. When you don't feel at home in the Now, no matter where you go, you will carry unease with you. The division of life into past, present, and future is mind-made and ultimately illusory. Past and future are thought forms, mental abstractions. The past can only be remembered Now. What you remember is an event that took place in the Now, and you remember it Now. The future, when it comes, is the Now. So the only thing that is real, the only thing there ever is *is* the Now." (Eckhart Tolle: Stillness Speaks) [128]

43. NO RESISTANCE

Is our challenge a question about Ignorance, Misunderstanding? Or is it rather a question of Willingness, resistance, escape, intention, ego, selfishness, and fear?

In the first case, the answer will be teaching, understanding, dialogue. In the latter case, the answer is rather one of right attitude: honesty, observation, discovery, insight, self knowledge, openness, willingness, Acceptance of Who you are and What is.

Probably we need both: Understanding and Acceptance. I am inclined to think that Understanding in principle is prior in time, with Acceptance following. But this Acceptance (willingness, experience, confirmation) is then necessary for being mature to gain new Understanding (insight, new awareness). Thus Acceptance and Understanding take turns, both paving way for the other.

There is an alternative way of seeing this.

Instead of going for many gradual insights, you might be more direct and look for the very core of the matter. If you are lucky, you may discover your wilfulness to resist What is (or what happens). The solution then is intellectually very simple, leaving you only with the challenge of Acceptance: "No Resistance!".

Zen saying

"The basic function of each being is expanding and contracting. Expanded beings are permeative; contracted beings are dense and impermeative. Therefore each of us, alone or in combination, may appear as space, energy, or mass, depending on the ratio of expansion to contraction chosen, and what kind of vibrations each of us expresses by alternating expansion and contraction. Each being controls his own vibrations. A completely expanded being is space. Since expansion is permeative, we can be in the "same space" with one or more other expanded beings. In fact, it is possible for all the entities in the universe to be one space. We experience expansion as awareness, comprehension, understanding, or whatever we wish to call it. When we are completely expanded, we have a feeling of total awareness, of being one with all life. At that level we have no resistance to any vibrations or interactions of other beings. It is timeless bliss, with unlimited choice of consciousness, perception, and feeling."

(Thaddeus Golas: The Lazy Man's Guide to Enlightenment) [44]

44. ILLUSIONS

Common sense, and especially idealistic belief systems, address the most precious, central, basic, dearly, human, holy, respectful Values we know. Zen claims they are Illusions. Furthermore, it is said that the one who has been misled must get out of it himself. And who is really not capable of doing it (!). Because no one exists (personality, ego) to do anything! This is an impressive collection of absurdities. Fortunately, and this seems to be the only way out, nothing has to be done, because there never was a real Problem, neither in the beginning, nor now.

The whole task, all the striving, all the worries, have been illusions, a Nightmare, a bad dream. Upon wakening up, everything is like before and has been so all the time and luckily, everything is just fine.

Zen saying

"I have never experienced a stressful feeling that wasn't caused by attaching to an untrue thought. Behind every uncomfortable feeling, there's a thought that isn't true for us. "The wind shouldn't be blowing". "My husband should agree with me". We think the thought that argues with reality, then we have a stressful feeling, and then we act on that feeling, creating more stress for ourselves. Rather than understand the original cause, a thought, we try to change our stressful feelings by looking outside ourselves. We try to change someone else, or we reach for sex, food, alcohol, drugs, or money to find temporary comfort and the illusion of control." (Byron, Katie: Loving What Is) [79]

45. REALITY

Liberation means consciousness development, a new kind of awareness. (Although it is actually a return to confidence in the original state of mind).

The only way is through self observation over a long period of time. Any kind of meditation, formal or informal, is highly beneficial. Probably necessary, too. Most people first need to really know and experience the calm, natural state of mind, with no thoughts or a calm floating stream of thoughts. There is a corresponding relaxation of bodily tensions as well. Deviance from this state – deviance is the default for everybody – will then act as a pointer for you that something could have been better in the current situation, something is misunderstood.

One may either reflect on such past experiences (retroactively), or even better – proactively observe yourself while meditating, while acting, interacting, thinking (mostly worrying!), planning/preparing in daily life. Look and see if the message (pointers) suggested here holds for you. It has only value if you find it somehow to be valid for you. If not, throw it away, if it is of any value, use it and then throw it away. Move on.

Zen saying

"For a start, let's note how far we can get with what's beyond all reasonable doubt. I'm referring to the fact that our central Emptiness (call it what we will: Void, Clarity, Spirit, Awake Capacity, Conscious No-thingness, or simply What's-now-taking-in-this-printing) is stripped of all traces and kinds of ownership, wiped clean of every personal label and distinguishing mark, of any indication of grade or status. It belongs to and is equally at home on all hierarchical levels. Manifestly What sees Itself here as Clarity is neither my Clarity, nor your Clarity, nor his or her Clarity, nor it's Clarity, but *the* Clarity, indivisible, universal. As indicated on our sketch-map of the First Person Singular, it's the Central Non-Being that lies at the Core of the countless beings it's forever giving rise to.

In other words, when you see into the Reality at your Centre, into What those countless regional appearances of yours are appearances of, you do so as none other than that all-embracing Reality itself. You do so as me and for me, and as and for everyone else as well. In fact your enlightenment is no different from and none other than the Buddha's, which – according to an ancient tradition – necessarily involved the enlightenment of all sentient beings of every grade and era. It's a tradition that's way ahead of our time, and one that sounds a timely warning. Though 'my' enlightenment is so obviously not mine, (no truly enlightened being sees itself surrounded by endarkened beings) my 'ego' says it is mine. Therefore let me tread cautiously as I venture into the field of enlightenment. Let me never forget that it's a minefield in both senses, and vigilance is essential if I'm not to be blown ego-sky-high."

(Douglas E. Harding: "To Be and not to be, that is the answer")
60

46. WHO AM I?

"The Void, or much ado about Nothing". Here comes a Zen short story about Persons, Things and Nothingness.

Sometime, Somebody met Someone Somewhere. Somebody knew that he himself was Nobody. Now he discovered that Someone really was himself, which could only mean that Someone also was Nobody.

Consequently, Nobody met Nobody. At that point, they could only laugh at the whole get together. Yet, neither Nobody nor Nobody knows what will happen next. Everything may happen. When Nothing turns into Everything, that's quite Something, as far as I can see. Who are You?

Zen saying

"No matter how vociferously I declare that I'm really based on and living from the human being that you see, I'm really based on and living from the Divine Being that you don't see, that I really am at Centre. I have to Be Right Here about Myself before I can be wrong there about myself!

No matter how negative my feelings about you and how bad my behaviour, the fact is that I give my life, my very being, for you. How could I possibly take you on without taking myself off, or see you without unseeing me? How can I undermine those negative feelings and that bad behaviour more radically than by seeing they have no real foundation?

No matter how distant I believe the stars are, and all those other objects near and far, the only way I can be in receipt of them is to abolish their distance, to coincide with them. I must have them here before I can dispatch them to what I call their proper places." (Douglas E. Harding: "To Be and not to be, that is the answer") [60]

47. NOTHINGNESS/EMPTINESS

If we are spontaneous by nature, with thinking as only another spontaneous specialised activity, then the Nothingness or Emptiness from which everything arises, must be "very productive". We lose ourselves, our personality, our pretended doings, but we gain a world. We lose our ego, but gain a conscious universe. We lose our social self, with all its comparisons between ourselves and others, all the self-esteem, all the self-blame, but discover the unity of one's Self in return.

Zen saying

"Empty and nihilistic as it may sound, this recognition of total nakedness and transparency is a joy beyond all telling, for what is empty is not reality itself but all that seems to block us light.

Old P'ang requires nothing in the world:
All is empty with him, even a seat he has not,
For absolute Emptiness reigns in his household;
How empty indeed it is with no treasures!
When the sun is risen, he walks through Emptiness,
When the sun sets, he sleeps in Emptiness;

Sitting in Emptiness he sings his empty songs,
And his empty songs reverberate through Emptiness.

To name or symbolize the joyous content of this emptiness is always to say too much, to put, as they say in Zen, legs upon the snake. For in Buddhist philosophy emptiness *(sunyata)* denotes the most solid and basic reality, though it is called empty because it never becomes an *object* of knowledge. This is because, being common to all related terms, figure and ground, solid and space, motion and rest, it is never seen in contrast with anything else and thus is never seen as an object. It may be called the fundamental reality or substance of the world only by analogy, for strictly speaking reality is known by contrast with unreality, and substance or stuff by contrast with shape or with empty space." (Alan W. Watts: Nature, Man and Woman) [136]

48.   ENLIGHTENMENT/AWAKENING/LIBERATION

Since liberation or enlightenment is a kind of returning Home to the natural state of spontaneity or open mind, this also gives us the clue to the end of seeking. Enlightenment is not "found" or "attained", you find yourself and you even discover that you were not really lost at any time, it "only" looked that way.

In all seeking then, the Questions are themselves symptoms of the problem itself. They are therefore also the key to the Answers, which are not really answers, but insight politely (or bluntly, as some Zen masters prefer) pointing back to the questions as artificial, misunderstood, self-constructed, misleading, self-conceiting. In short, the questions and the problems they represent are virtual. Since this is unknown, it is unconscious and the problems appear very real. This is the common virtuality of our everyday lives. (Though the problems are artificial, the consequences of believing in them are real and destructive, as demonstrated by all kinds of conflicts on individual, group and national levels).

The support to the Asker will then be to gently redirect his or her attention back to the question and themselves, back to the asking. Who is asking? Why? What does the question mean. What is the motive? The reason for asking may be different from what it appears. May be just the opposite. A clue to use here is to look for the difference between what seems to be and what is. Since the Answer resides in the Asker, dialogue is so widely applied by many gurus. (But usually very boring for others to read about, for the very reason that both the problem and the answer are so individually founded. Hang-ups mean a lot to the person in question but are hardly of universal interest).

Zen saying

"What *is* enlightenment?

Enlightenment is finding that there is nothing to find. Enlightenment is to come to know that there is nowhere to go. Enlightenment is the understanding that this is all, that this is perfect, that this is it. Enlightenment is not an achievement, it is an understanding that there is nothing to achieve, nowhere to go. You are already there, you have never been away. You cannot be away from there. God has never been missed. Maybe you have forgotten, that's all. Maybe you have fallen asleep, that's all. Maybe you have gotten lost in many, many dreams, that's all, but you are there. God is your very being. So the first thing is, don't think about enlightenment as a goal, it is not. It is not a goal; it is not some thing that you can desire. And if you desire it you will not get it. In desiring a thousand and one things, by and by you come to understand that all desire is futile. Each desire lands you in frustration; each desire again and again throws you into a ditch. This has been happening for millions of years but again you start hoping, again you start thinking that this new desire that is arising, sprouting in you, will maybe lead you to paradise. That this will give you what *you* have longed for, that it will fulfil you. Again and again hope arises.

Enlightenment is when all hope disappears. Enlightenment is disappearance of hope." (Osho: Zen: The Path of Paradox) [106]

49. THOUGHTS

Thinking is mainly worrying! Thoughts are fear. This may seem outrageous, because thinking is one of our very most precious values and capabilities. It is regarded as *the* human characteristic, both in common understanding and in the sciences. The value of planning and systematic thought is well known and not at stake here. The everyday stream of thoughts occupying or lurking in our heads more than 90% of the day is another matter.

Don't take this, neither as rubbish nor at face value. Look for yourself. Observe. How often are your thoughts regret about the past or worry about the future? Secondly, ponder the fruitlessness of the worries. Do they solve the problem or are they rather a big part of the problem itself when there is a challenge coming to you in the future?

Zen saying

"Thought is a distraction. Thought is a disturbance. It is only when thought is again not there that we come into contact with the ultimate. If one thinks about it one can think and think and think, but it eludes thought; it goes on slipping out of it. And then, seeing that thinking is not leading anywhere, it stops on its own accord. If one really goes on thinking to the very end, a state of non-thinking happens automatically. This end of thinking comes finally and naturally, that's what Zen proposes". (Osho: Zen: The Path of Paradox) [106]

50. DEVELOPMENT

Here is a warning for all interested in liberation or self development. Our Western culture is extremely achievement oriented. Every activity is aiming at improvement, doing better or competing. Liberation requires a genuine change in that attitude. This also goes for the desire for liberation itself. The more you strive, the farther you are from success. The more you accept the way you are, the faster you'll progress. Obviously a paradoxical situation...

Here is another warning. We speak of "development", "stages in consciousness development" and "levels of understanding". There *is* a progress in the understanding and awareness of yourself-in-the-world. However, the ultimate "liberated" or "enlightened" state is no advanced state or superior way of functioning. It is rather a return to the innocent, natural spontaneous, open mind of a child, now with the conscious confidence that this is the natural state of mind. "Zen mind is ordinary mind". "Before Enlightenment I was eating, drinking and carrying wood. After Enlightenment I was eating, drinking and carrying wood."

A return Home or awakening after a long detour through virtual reality in a dream with plenty of nightmares and fighting against windmills. A journey where you don't arrive before you see that you never really left Home, in the first place...[154]

Zen saying

"My point is, do we turn into seekers, or is there a force which turns certain people into seekers and completely ignores many others? If it is a force which turns people into seekers, why should those people consider themselves responsible for the seeking? If you have been turned into a seeker, is it not reasonable to accept that it is the responsibility of the force to take you where it will, to make you do that kind of *sadhana* which is necessary for you at that moment? Is it necessary to consider and wonder whether what you are doing at any moment is right or wrong, correct or incorrect? Who is it that can be improved?" (Ramesh S. Balsekar: Consciousness Speaks) [8]

51. FREE WILL

The Bad News is:

There is no free will. For instance, for self improvement, development, personal change, responsibility. Accordingly there is no reason to blame either yourself or other people for not being better than you or they are (!). [61,62,63,64,154]

The Good News is:

It is not necessary to have free will. Because there is nothing which needs to be changed. When you discover, see, feel that you have "responsibility" (!) (in the sense of ownership), that you will/want/make the very same problems you denounce (do not recognise, fight against), then you have already changed and the world will improve and be different.

To be spontaneous, requires that you know, trust and are willing to let go of all the control. It is as easy and as difficult as that. "The Way is through the open door. Why is it that so few go through?" [90]

Zen saying

"And if we can't choose our thoughts maybe we can't choose our actions either. When that's clear, all sense of guilt or pride melts away. This doesn't mean that we now become serial killers or terrorists. We continue to live as before but all those habits of criticizing ourselves and others can fall away. Imagine how many internal dialogues would disappear. If there is no free choice, it is also clear that every moment of our life up until now has been absolutely appropriate. Not one step could have been taken differently. Everything you apparently did couldn't have been any different! We are just actors in a movie, acting and reacting according to our conditionings. Our programmes just respond to the circumstances. When we see that we can't manage our thoughts, there is a sense of freedom that arises, because now we see that everything is just happening as it is happening." (Jan Kersschot: This Is It) [81]

CHAPTER 6

THE ZEN QUIZ "MY WORLD"

A TEST YOU CAN USE TO DISCOVER WHO YOU ARE NOW

BACKGROUND AND EXPLANATION

The validity of this inquiry is based on your own reporting of what type of interests and concerns you are focused on. Here you are the only expert in the whole world and potentially a very reliable one too.

Many of the questions or rather statements which you are asked to agree or disagree with, may trigger your reflection and perhaps change your previous understanding. That is just fine of course, nothing is better than that. The purpose is not necessarily the test results but increased awareness.

Don't be afraid to find out who you are now. This is totally safe and there is a lot of fun and adventure ahead of you. In fact, being aware and knowing yourself may seem frightening to some but it is the safest activity in the world. Becoming more aware, secure and perhaps self confident has never hurt anybody. Enjoy!

INSTRUCTIONS

Below you will find statements about the world, other people and yourself.

No statements are right or wrong; they represent different viewpoints or perspectives on the world around us. The idea behind this Quiz is that *your world* reflects what *you are*.

For each group of the 4 statements, please select the one you like best or think is most true.

Scoring and interpretation of the results will follow later.

THE ZEN QUIZ "MY WORLD"

A QUIZ FOR ZEN PSYCHOLOGY

(Copyright Stein Gaarder. Version 1, 2020-07-10)

INSTRUCTIONS: *For each group of 4 statements, please select the one you like best or think is most true.*

____ You are responsible for your own destiny.
____ Our responsibility is to improve the world, the people included.
____ We should try to live in the Here and Now.
____ Everyone is living in the Here and Now, there is no option.

____ "Survival of the fittest" should be applied also to modern mankind.
____ Everyone can and should improve themselves personally.
____ There are no methods, not even trying to follow no methods.
____ Man is born neither Good nor Evil, and should be raised properly.

____ Spontaneity requires unconditional trust in letting things happen.
____ I believe in the existence of Good and Evil forces.
____ Some spiritual techniques/systems are better than others.
____ A better world is only a matter of right attitudes and effort.

____ Cooperation is sometimes more important
than competition.

____ I believe in "An eye for eye, tooth for tooth".

____ The potential for spiritual improvement is huge
or unlimited.

____ There is no ego, really.

____ Self improvement is a typical ego activity.

____ Achievement is the fruit of your efforts.

____ Bad behaviour is due to lack of self control,
more than to low moral.

____ All people need to be guided, through politics
and/or religion.

____ All people need guidance, but it is more important
How you give help than What you do.

____ No act is really our own doing.

____ To be honest, there are the good guys and
there are the bad guys.

____ Right decision is more a question of moral than
of understanding.

____ There is something wrong with me, but that goes
for most people.

____ My perceived physical and social environment
is my consciousness, it is me.

____ Moral behaviour is a matter of right decisions
more than of understanding.

____ That you fight for the good causes is more important
than the way you are behaving.

___ Terrorism can be overcome by force alone.
___ The right causes (goals) are more important
than the right intentions.
___ Trying to solve problems is itself the problem.
___ Most thoughts are rational, and not worries.

___ Conflict and violence is natural and necessary
for the development of man and culture.
___ Development is much a question of strengthening
the self or ego.
___ You do not have to change or improve.
___ There is a natural conflict between Right and Wrong,
Good and Evil.

___ Without my thinking ego I would lose the
necessary control.
___ I am neither determined by circumstances,
nor have free will.
___ Right religion and right politics would solve
most of the conflicts in the world.
___ People need rewards and they should be given
help according to needs, not only efforts.

___ Spontaneity is the natural state of mind or flow
of things.
___ "When the going gets tough, the tough gets going".
___ I am more focused on my own development than
the improvement/correction of others.
___ Egoistic behaviour is primitive and should
be punished.

____ Improvement of others is more important than acceptance.

____ The meaning of life is to have achieved something.

____ Discovering that you *will* your problems is a great insight.

____ Personal development usually requires a strong will and endurance.

____ If the Ends are important enough, they justify the Means.

____ My questions are a symptom of the problem itself.

____ Conflict and violence is unnatural and should be eliminated or prevented whenever possible.

____ Self control is a virtue, but the control of people or behaviour is less so.

____ Improvement is more important than Spontaneity.

____ There is a basic conflict between cultural development and natural environment.

____ Ignorance and violence is natural in the sense of things being as they are.

____ Wrong attitudes are mostly due to selfishness or greed.

____ The meaning of life is to be useful for others.

____ Attack is the best self-defense.

____ I practise being more in the Here-and-Now.

____ What *is*, is more important than what *should* be.

CHAPTER 7

CONSCIOUSNESS, STAGES AND DEVELOPMENT

CONSCIOUSNESS DEVELOPMENT: A PSYCHOLOGICAL SUPPLEMENT TO ZEN

One of the central themes of Zen is the perfection of Nature. This includes human nature and every individual person with our seeming shortcomings.

Zen focuses on the genuine nature of our minds, our real selves. Perceived problems are of a more superficial, virtual nature, shadowing the perfect nature underneath. There is consequently no need for improvement or development, the challenge is to look behind or through the cinematic screen of nightmares and reveal or re-discover the forgotten land of bliss and harmony. For the persons involved however, their problems (everything from violent conflicts to dissatisfaction, worries, insecurity, fear or depression) are real enough and play a substantial part of most peoples lives. This situation is by no means a transitory state of affairs, a passing storm expected to calm down by itself. It runs through generation after generation and there is little unanimous evidence of any improvement or development. There may even be an increased level of stress and frustration over time. Inspite of thousands of years with culture, experience, technology, politics and religions. [22,112,118,130,136,139,144]

If we undertake the experiment to look at the Zen principles from a psychological point of view, something interesting happens. Zen's well-formulated and now familiar problems of everyday life suddenly display themselves in a relatively simple and systematic developmental perspective. Not necessarily developmental in the outward, cultural or political sense but as *development of consciousness*, that is our perception of ourselves, other people and the environment. And that is not all. The developmental process, still exclusively constituent of Zen principles, also reveals the key to progress, in that each stage provides the solution to the preceding stage (or dissolution, as Zen would prefer).

MISUNDERSTANDINGS: THE ROOT OF PERSONAL PROBLEMS AND SOCIAL CONFLICTS

Fundamental in Zen is the perspective of seeing existential problems as primarily due to Misunderstandings, with a capital M. The problems are of course not limited to intellectual misperceptions, but the focus is on understanding/insight rather than attitudes, emotions or bodily dysfunctions. The Misunderstandings evolve around the perception of oneself in relation to the universe, the "me" as related to the "not-me". Each Misunderstanding represents a mistake, a disharmony in this primal relationship. Please consider how universal the me/not me relationship is: All our behaviour, perceptions, thinking, intentions, motives, feelings, you name it, are based on how we draw the line between me and not-me, between what we like or dislike, familiar/unfamiliar, identify with/keep distance, fight/support, fear/love.

As William James pointed out long ago, we all draw the line differently. This has major consequences. We draw the line to the best of our ability of course, but at any moment the result is a Me and a Not-me.

The Not-me is everything else apart from me, the people around me, the physical environment, the external world. In the same manner that the me is Me, the external world then becomes the World, with a capital W. And it is this World that I relate to, also when my perception is more or less mistaken and I am met with disharmony and confusion. The Me tries to handle the World as best as it can. What more can you demand than the best of ability and intentions? If anything fails, and it does, the World is probably wrong and we must try to change it. This inclination to improve the world is in reality of a conservative nature although announced as being progressive. Projecting the blame outwards is a much used self protection. Or, as we sometimes admit, perhaps we should try something different or even change ourselves. However, we are then still trying to fix something "Other", we have just externalised (and alienated) our shortcoming and want to fix that one as well. Consequently the "ourselves" is still an outward projection, disregarding and concealing that we (I, my ego) re-create the problem every moment. This would have been a completely static state of affairs were it not for the changing nature of consciousness. Consciousness is not a passive observer; it changes whatever is the object from moment to moment. It seeks, selects, considers, and creates. And is itself being changed (influenced) by whatever happens. At rather rare times, when we are confronted with obstacles in the World, we become aware of the me/not-me distinction. Then a change is likely to happen. We draw the line a little differently, we include a little more of the World, assimilates so the external becomes internal and there is less conflict. The Misunderstanding has turned into Understanding and we have reached a new small stage in consciousness. This is improvement or Development (with a capital D). We shall see that this simple principle may be applied to all the stages of human behaviour, from the most egoistic and power-oriented attitudes to the most compassionate and spontaneous ways of living.

CONSCIOUSNESS IS DEVELOPMENT

The psychological approach probably disagrees with Zen on one important aspect. Zen usually advocates (there are different schools in this matter) the sudden and complete insight from any current state of confusion (yours as well as mine) directly to the fully liberated state (satori or enlightenment). There is no gradual improvement or development there. And truly, trying is lying. Trying to improve is just another game within the ego-centred activities, in this case the game of self improvement, using (and strengthening) the ego to get rid of the ego. However, the psychological alternative does not necessarily have to enter that trap. (But does absolutely need this most appropriate warning from Zen, and keep it constantly in mind). In any life situation of a particular person (in any state or at any stage) there is the possibility of increasing the awareness by incorporating (assimilating) the seemingly alien, external World, the seemingly not-me. This happens suddenly and spontaneously and is perfect for the moment. But it is usually a very limited experience as compared to the person's potential other life experiences. It is thus a *development* in the right direction and results in a somewhat more wholesome state. When this continues over a long time, a certain degree of perceived unity between me and not-me is attained for most of the persons behaviour, thus being characteristic for him or her, then we may say this person usually functions on that particular "level". However, it is probably wise to focus as little as possible on "levels", "stages", "advanced", "development" and the like, due to the ego-pride. Having once got the hang of it, everyone can quite easily recognize the type of me/not-me relationship that is happening in each situation, whether one is observing oneself or others. Having this awareness, the understanding is never forgotten and will go on in its own pace by itself. Being aware of (conscious) the natural (but slow, up to then) consciousness development is by itself actually one of the many states or steps on the same track. Please note what we just achieved: "being aware (conscious) of consciousness development". Suddenly the development of consciousness became within our "powers" (!). Not as a technique but as a new kind of awareness or understanding. At this stage we are invited to take a deliberate attitude to our consciousness itself. Not to control it but to trust spontaneity. Not to change it but willingly accept every moment. Neither to judge nor to ignore, just looking beyond or through the "good" and "bad". No Resistance. No Doing. Trusting what happens. Your action and re-actions will be just fine, more appropriate in the total context than you may believe. Even when they are not deliberately planned as "yours". Especially then. Only then.

THE PRIMAL MISTAKE AND THE WAY OUT

The starting point is the drawing of the line between me and not-me, between Me and the World, Me and the Other. The very act of drawing this line is the Mistake, with a capital M, but a necessary and natural part of consciousness development. Drawing the line separates the organism from the surroundings, from the universe outside. In reality there is a unity, there was and there will be. We can *only try* to divide and then *believe* in it. And trying and believing we do. However, drawing the line creates an apparent disharmony because we separate (or try to) what is really one. We create an artificial division and have to pay the consequences. The Empire strikes back. The closer to "ourselves" we draw the line, and the more strongly we believe in it, the harsher are the consequences and the feeling of disharmony. The narrower our definition of ourselves is, the more territory is left to the external, alien world.

The more widely we perceive ourselves and the more accepting we are, the less is left for alienation, "otherness". There is a correspondence between WHAT we believe is wrong and HOW we want to cope with it. This characterises each level.

Within each level we may conveniently envisage 3 phases or stages of development:

1. *Experience* over time that what we are doing does not work too well. This may go on for a long, long time. Examples: negative feedback from other people or from our self-perceived shortcomings, repetitive frustrations, general dissatisfaction.

2. *Understanding*, or sensing, why it does not work and that we may be doing it the wrong way. Examples: Learning, introspection, trial and error, questioning.

3. *Discover*, actively experiment and see that when we do something differently, it may work better. Examples: Awareness, observation, insight.

At every step, there is a challenge between the Apparent (the Virtual) and the Real.

The real (undivided) world provides feedback and pointers, but receptiveness on behalf of the receiver is required. Generally one may say that the development goes from density, control and conflict at the lowest level – to space, lightness and harmony at the other end. From focus on the outer world to the inner. From alienation and paranoia to sharing. From fear to trust.

From ego centration to decentration. From concepts to spontaneity. From control to liberation.

THE LEVELS OF CONSCIOUSNESS

At the lowest level then, there is the sharpest division, the most blatant splitting of the universe in two, and the most antagonistic relationship between the two halves. This level of consciousness may be called "Dualism". (It corresponds I believe, pretty well with the mainstream of the well-known philosophical and psychological theories of dualism).

At this level there is a strong feeling of there being something wrong with the World. And our way of dealing with it calls for Control. WHAT is wrong = the World. HOW we cope with it = Control. The WHATs and HOWs may be used to characterise each level of development.

Gradually, over a long time, one realizes that the focus of concern should be people rather than the external world (including political and social systems). Without sufficient knowledge, understanding, right attitudes, motivation, guidance, ethics, the political systems and even agreements will not work. So the focus shifts from systems (external world) to people, cooperation and helping each other. The WHAT = People. The HOW = Help. This we may call the level of Humanism.

At the next level we become aware of our own role and responsibility for a better relationship with other people and the world at large. Consequently one focuses more on self development. The WHAT = Oneself. The HOW = Develop (improve). This is the level of Self Development.

At the final level one has had a lot of experience with "working on oneself does not work". One starts looking at a more fundamental level and one turns one's attention towards consciousness itself.

The WHAT = Consciousness.

The HOW = Observe (being aware, accepting observation, meditation, mindfulness).

We have entered the level of Seeking. Here is a summary of the levels with their respective keywords:

	LEVEL 1 Dualism	LEVEL 2 Humanism	LEVEL 3 Self Development	LEVEL 4 Seeking
WHAT	The World	People	Oneself	Consciousness
HOW	Control	Help	Develop	Observe

In Zen Psychology we apply Zen as a guidance for awareness and progress from one level to another. Basically Zen is only interested in getting beyond all the stages. Typically Zen scriptures and teachers address the level of Seeking where there is a high degree of understanding (self insight) but where the individuals are nevertheless lost (and stuck) on their spiritual path. One may assume that there is no or little interest in Zen at the levels of Dualism and Humanism (!). From a dualistic viewpoint Zen may seem naïve and unrealistic. From a humanist perspective Zen might seem too laissez-faire or even cynical. At the level of Self Development Zen may be one of the many possible "solutions" that one stumbles across while looking for improvements. However, Zen is not likely to win the competition of offering a quick fix. But who knows, everything in due time.

The 51 common zense items in chapter 5 have been presented in a sequence corresponding to the level of consciousness development they represent. The detailed sequence within one level is not to be taken literally, but the items are grouped as Dualism, Humanism, Self development and Seeking, in that order. The following table reveals this progress. Interest in or preoccupation with certain types of life questions corresponds to a characteristic level of development. Some items will thus have much more significance for some people than for others. "Lower level" items may be understood but seem less interesting while "higher level" items may appear both obscure and less interesting. (It should be noted that the labelling of the items may easily introduce some ambiguity when taken as one single name. The precision increases with the explanatory text (in Chapter 5) and with its position in the following table).

COMMON ZENSE ITEMS
ZEN PSCYHOLOGY APPLIED TO
COMMON SENSE AND EVERYDAY LIFE

	LEVEL 1 Dualism	LEVEL 2 Humanism	LEVEL 3 Self Development	LEVEL 4 Seeking
WHAT	The World	People	Oneself	Consciousness
HOW	Control	Help	Develop	Observe
COMMON ZENSE ITEMS				
	Dualism	Dissatisfied	Self-development	Liberation
	Stress	Belief in systems	Concepts	Appearance
	Fear	Achievement	Meditation	Paradoxes
	Aggression	Something wrong	Seeking	Exercises
	Depression	Belief hope doubt	Ego	Spontaneity
	Conflict with the world	Right / wrong	Consciousness / awareness	No resistance
	Religion / psychology / politics	Ethics	Improvement	Illusions
	Zen	Life quality	Zen Commandments	Reality
	Good / bad	Neurosis	Pretending	Who am I?
		Frustration	No theory	Nothingness / emptiness
		Virtual reality	Acceptance	Enlightenment / awakening / liberation
		Happiness	Control oneself	Thoughts
		Nothing wrong with you	Peace of mind	Development
			Psychotherapy	Free will
			No doing	

YOUR WORLD IS YOU

Your perceptions are a representation of what kind of world YOU are living in. That is most significant. In the Zen quiz "My World" you will find that some of the questions and topics will be very familiar and some very strange. That is just the point. Everyone has his or her highly personal profile regarding the perception of the world. There are 4 "levels" or qualitative different ways of perceiving, or 4 different worlds, if you want. HOWEVER, there are no right or wrong answers except that they should reflect what you really identify with and NOT what you think should be the right answer. What YOU think or feel is you-here-and-now. *Furthermore, understanding of yourself is the only starting point for any kind of awareness or self development.* That is why you will find this simple Quiz useful for finding who you are, right now. Everything apart from awareness is self deception, postponements or excuses. This is also an option, of course. Everything goes.

Taken together, the statements will add up to a certain perspective, a certain focus, which is your typical way of perceiving things, which again is the typical "you", although not in the most fundamental sense. The results are grouped in a few broad categories, describing your personal profile. I suggest that you look for what is most to your own liking rather than guessing what could be the best answer. In Zen they say that what *Is*, is what really matters. Not what *Should* be.

NB! There is one big bias in this self inventory. Applying your knowledge of Zen (or Zen Psychology) you may in a theoretical way guess what is supposed to be the most "advanced" answers. It is therefore wise to remember that you are not fooling anybody apart from yourself. The real test is to honestly compare the statements with your own experience, especially those experiences where you feel discomfort, dislike, regret, fear, conflict or anger. In short, include also the dark side of the world or, of yourself.

On the following two pages the quiz questions are grouped according to each of the four levels of consciousness development. Your own preferred items will together display your profile as compared to this scale. An interpretation of the results and a "facit" for aggregating your score is offered a little later on. Just count the number of As, Bs, Cs and Ds you get to see which level most represents you.

THE FOUR LEVELS OF CONSCIOUSNESS WITH THEIR REPRESENTATIVE PERCEPTIONS OF THE WORLD

Level 1 = Dualism

> = Focus on the external world
> = Control and Fear

A1   You are responsible for your own destiny.

A2   "Survival of the fittest" should be applied also to modern mankind.

A3   I believe in the existence of Good and Evil forces.

A4   I believe in "An eye for eye, tooth for tooth".

A5   Achievement is the fruit of your efforts.

A6   To be honest, there are the good guys and there are the bad guys.

A7   Moral behaviour is a matter of the right decisions more than of understanding.

A8   Terrorism can be overcome by force alone.

A9   Conflict and violence is natural and necessary for the development of man and culture.

A10   Right religion and right politics would solve most of the conflicts in the world.

A11   "When the going gets tough, the tough get going".

A12   The meaning of life is to have achieved something.

A13   If the Ends are important enough, they justify the Means.

A14   There is a basic conflict between cultural development and the natural environment.

A15   Attack is the best self-defense.

Level 2 = Humanism

> = Focus on other people.
>
> = Reforming and Helping

B1 Our responsibility is to improve the world, the people included.

B2 Man is born neither Good nor Evil, and should be raised properly.

B3 A better world is only a matter of right attitudes and effort.

B4 Cooperation is sometimes more important than competition.

B5 All people need to be guided, through politics and/or religion.

B6 Making the right decision is more a question of morality than of understanding.

B7 The fact that you fight for good causes is more important than the way you behave.

B8 The right causes (goals) are more important than good intentions.

B9 There is a natural conflict between Right and Wrong, Good and Evil.

B10 People need rewards and they should be given help according to needs, not only efforts.

B11 Egoistic behaviour is primitive and should be punished.

B12 Improvement of others is more important than acceptance.

B13 Conflict and violence is unnatural and should be eliminated or prevented whenever possible.

B14 Wrong attitudes are mostly due to selfishness or greed.

B15 The meaning of life is to be useful for others.

Level 3 = Self development

= Focus on oneself

= Self-hate and Development

C1   We should try to live in the Here and Now.

C2   Everyone can and should improve
themselves personally.

C3   Some spiritual techniques/systems are better than others.

C4   The potential for spiritual improvement
is huge or unlimited.

C5   Bad behaviour is more due to lack of
self control than low morals.

C6   All people need guidance, but it is more important
How you give help than What you do.

C7   There is something wrong with me,
but that goes for most people.

C8   Most thoughts are rational, and not worries.

C9   Development is much a question of
strengthening the self or ego.

C10 Without my thinking ego I would
lose the necessary control.

C11 I am more focused on my own development
than the improvement/correction of others.

C12 Personal development usually requires
strong will and endurance.

C13 Self control is a virtue, but the control
of people or behaviour is less so.

C14 Improvement is more important than Spontaneity.

C15 I practise being more in the Here and Now.

Level 4 = Seeking

= Focus on Consciousness

= Seeking and Observing

D1 Everyone is living in the Here and Now, there is no option.

D2 There are no methods, not even the attempt to follow no methods.

D3 Spontaneity requires unconditional trust in letting things happen.

D4 There is no ego, really.

D5 Self improvement is a typical ego activity.

D6 No act is really our own doing.

D7 My perceived physical and social environment *is* my consciousness, it is me.

D8 Trying to solve problems is itself the problem.

D9 You do not have to change or improve.

D10 I am neither determined by circumstances, nor have free will.

D11 Spontaneity is the natural state of mind or flow of things.

D12 Discovering that you *will* your problems is a great insight.

D13 My questions are a symptom of the problem itself.

D14 Ignorance and violence is natural in the sense of things being as they are.

D15 What *is*, is more important than what *should* be.

SCORING AND INTERPRETATION
OF THE QUIZ RESULTS

First, a little warning. This is not a standardised test of spiritual maturity, just an illustration.

There is the pitfall that one may have an **intellectual** knowledge about 'higher' level items without really **living** with them oneself. Thus if the Quiz is answered only theoretically, it may be worthwhile to go back and look at the items from a more personal and authentic point of view.

This is how the rating works:

The scoring consists simply of assigning a number from 1-4 to your selected items, according to which level (1-4) the item belongs. Thus, selecting an item belonging to the first level "Dualism", receives 1 point, items from level 2 receive 2 points, level 3 receives 3 points, level 4 receives 4 points for each item. Then add up your points. Since there are 15 items at each level, we get the following most **typical average** for each particular level:

Dualism = 15 points (1x15), Humanism = 30 points (2x15), Self development = 45 points (3x15) and Seeking = 60 points (4x15).

Consequently, you can compare your result with the typical average representing each level (or mode of viewing the world). You will usually have selected items from several levels (due to variable life experiences and also possible ambiguities of the questions/items).

SOME IMPLICATIONS OF EVALUATING CONSCIOUSNESS

The Quiz may serve as an applied illustration of different world views, which are not merely viewpoints but represent how we perceive the world. Since these different *worlds* (literally meant) are very stable over years for most people (and usually over generations!), I believe it is important to recognize their fundamental significance. For example, in our generation it is common sense that most conflicts or disagreements may be sorted out, provided we just communicate. A great deal can be said in favour of dialogue (and it is a higher level than fighting!) but it may be wise to also be aware of the limitations of communication when people literally live in different worlds. This goes for the individual, personal level as well as the cultural level (society, political, religious). Many of the current international conflicts are surprisingly resistant to talks and good intentions from both sides of the table. You will probably find some of the "irrational" behaviour among your acquaintances and friends easier to understand and relate to, if you are aware there may be more fundamental differences than those rectified by information and communication. There is of course, no ready-made prescription for the alternative approaches. Questioning the assumption that everyone is living in the same world, is a start. It may call for more sophisticated and patient communication over a long time. It will usually imply a change of attitude and lots of reflection. But first of all, the main value of the Quiz depends on the awareness and interest it may trigger for each individual. Development, evolution, improvement, achievement, competition, are the highlights of success and happiness in most cultures. The mere knowledge about "higher" states of consciousness will probably be motivating for some, and provocative for others. But the awareness will by itself promote development if we are ready for it. Perhaps we are now prepared for facilitating the development of consciousness, gently and in a natural way.

The term Zen Psychology implies a little more conscious, systematic, public, provocative and modern promotion of the essence of Zen. The time may be right to adopt Zen to our more familiar, Western conditions and language. Not necessarily in order to de-mystify but to popularize a little and avoid the religious or alien Eastern roots which are unfamiliar to most of us. Psychology may work as one way for us to interpret the ancient and seemingly strange expressions of Zen. Some time in the future, discussions about our common sense may well turn out to be the most proper arena for Zen demonstrations. Many fundamentals of Common sense are turned upside down when Zen is recognized and thus appreciated as the very radical alternative it actually is.

If our time is not yet receptive to a more popular and psychological version of Zen, it will not do much harm anyway. It is well known in Zen that sometimes the longest way around may turn out to be the shortest way home.

ZEN PSYCHOLOGY IS JUST A START.
YOU ARE THE ONLY GURU THERE IS

The scope of this book is to identify just some of the main general differences between Zen, psychology and common sense. It does not really cover the practical implications and possibilities of Zen or Zen combined with our more familiar beliefs and traditions. *A lot of opportunities remain to be explored.* However, even a purely intellectual and superficial understanding of Zen principles may be very useful. For one thing, it is valuable just to know that many of our everyday worries and conflicts simply do not have substantial reality. That there are a lot of make believe problems that are unnecessary and a waste of time and for many people, a waste of a lifetime. This will trigger a self awareness and self observation which over time will provide insight. Zen also provides lots of hints regarding where to look or how to look. Further, we learn at the very beginning not to let this awareness increase our worries, because the very essence of it all is to accept yourself more, not less. Thirdly, if we seek prescriptions, exercises or help or therapy, it is wise to know that I am, have been and always will be, ultimately on my own. No guru or psychologist can really "give" you insight and liberation. It is your own journey inwards (and outwards, if we mean less self centered and more spontaneous). Finally, Zen also discloses the taboo that much of your troubles are of your own making, and guess what happens every time you experience that for yourself? If this is not enough, Zen even strongly insists that your problems or dissatisfaction are only seemingly real, that there never really was anything wrong with you, that you have been "liberated" all along. You have only not been aware of it because you have been told or have chosen to ignore or forget about it. The receptiveness and genuine interest in such matters is not entirely up to each one of us but depends upon life experience and present consciousness/awareness. Being spiritually ambitious is one of the big counter productive traps. Fortunately, Zen is extremely generous in the sense that self acceptance is THE highway to liberation. Whatever, whoever you are now (Now), is the only acceptance or insight that is required. The observant reader will have noticed that advocating different levels of consciousness development, runs the risk of fostering spiritual competitiveness, pride or ambition – and thus becoming counter productive. However, such ambitions and behaviour are easily detected (by others or preferably by yourself) as being typical ego-activities (if you know a little bit of Zen) and thus self defeating and harmless.

One last observation. All the stages, even level 4, represent at best *relative* truths, i.e. they are true relative to the misunderstandings of lower levels but not much more. Complete liberation goes beyond the statements, beyond all statements whatsoever. Liberation is not about What we should think or do, but How we may be and live.

"MY WORLD": QUIZ FACIT

A1   You are responsible for your own destiny.
B1   Our responsibility is to improve the
      world, the people included.
C1   We should try to live in the Here and Now.
D1   Everyone is living in the Here and
      Now, there is no option.

A2   "Survival of the fittest" should be applied also to
      modern mankind.
C2   Everyone can and should improve
      themselves personally.
D2   There are no methods, not even the
      attempt to follow no methods.
B2   Man is born neither Good nor Evil,
      and should be raised properly.

D3   Spontaneity requires unconditional
      trust in letting things happen.
A3   I believe in the existence of Good and Evil forces.
C3   Some spiritual techniques/systems are better than others.
B3   A better world is only a matter of
      right attitudes and effort.

B4   Cooperation is sometimes more
      important than competition.
A4   I believe in "An eye for eye, tooth for tooth".
C4   The potential for spiritual improvement
      is huge or unlimited.
D4   There is no ego, really.

D5   Self improvement is a typical ego activity.

A5   Achievement is the fruit of your efforts.

C5   Bad behaviour is more due to lack of
self control than low morals.

B5   All people need to be guided, through
politics and/or religion.

C6   All people need guidance, but it is more important
How you give help than What you do.

D6   No act is really our own doing.

A6   To be honest, there are the good guys
and there are the bad guys.

B6   Right decision is more a question of
moral than of understanding.

C7   There is something wrong with me,
but that goes for most people.

D7   My perceived physical and social environment
is my consciousness, it is me.

A7   Moral behaviour is a matter of right
decisions more than of understanding.

B7   That you fight for the good causes is more
important than the way you behave.

A8   Terrorism can be overcome by force alone.

B8   The right causes (goals) are more
important than the right intentions.

D8   Trying to solve problems is itself the problem.

C8   Most thoughts are rational, and not worries.

A9   Conflict and violence is natural and necessary
      for the development of man and culture.
C9   Development is very much a question
      of strengthening the self or ego.
D9   You do not have to change or improve.
B9   There is a natural conflict between Right
      and Wrong, Good and Evil.

C10   Without my thinking ego I would
      lose the necessary control.
D10   I am neither determined by
      circumstances, nor have free will.
A10   The right religion and politics would solve
      most of the conflicts in the world.
B10   People need rewards and they should be given
      help according to their needs, not only efforts.

D11   Spontaneity is the natural state of mind or flow of things.
A11   "When the going gets tough, the tough get going".
C11   I am more focused on my own development
      than the improvement/correction of others.
B11   Egoistic behaviour is primitive and should be punished.

B12   Improvement of others is more
      important than acceptance.
A12   The meaning of life is to have achieved something.
D12   Discovering that you *will* your
      problems, is a great insight.
C12   Personal development usually requires
      a strong will and endurance.

A13 If the Ends are important enough,
     they justify the Means.
D13 My questions are a symptom of the problem itself.
B13 Conflict and violence is unnatural and should be
     eliminated or prevented whenever possible.
C13 Self control is a virtue, but the control
     of people or behaviour is less so.

C14 Improvement is more important than Spontaneity.
A14 There is a basic conflict between cultural
     development and the natural environment.
D14 Ignorance and violence is natural in the
     sense of things being as they are.
B14 Wrong attitudes are mostly due to selfishness or greed.

B15 The meaning of life is to be useful for others.
A15 Attack is the best self-defense.
C15 I practise being more in the Here-and-Now.
D15 What *is*, is more important than what *should* be.

CHAPTER 8

CONCLUSION

SUMMING UP WHO IS ASKING?

As a basis for the discussion we used our common sense questions about life in general, and about others and ourselves, in particular. In a Zen perspective these questions and especially the insecure and worrying aspects of them, reflect to a very large degree Misunderstandings and negative feedback from the natural flow of events which we have tried to control but have instead disturbed. Such questions are "answered" by Zen, from a position which does not really has any "message", theory or prescription by itself but only neutralises the original question or problem. The misunderstood concepts are turned around, themselves being questioned and thus returned to the person who is asking. Fortunately, sometimes the questioner knows the answer and discovers that he or she is making up the problem. But usually they will still have new problems to offer. The result is a dialogue, which repeatedly and elaborately returns the attention and consciousness back to the person, back to the one who is asking. NB! It does not necessarily have to be a dialogue with another person, as in coaching. Once you have understood the principle of yourself creating the problems, you are welcome to observe, question and "transform" yourself! The dialogue with a guru, therapist or friend may well be substituted by your own observation and reflections. After all it is only *your* insight that matters.

Common sense has a set of basic Misunderstandings.

These may be counteracted by Zen (or Zen Psychology).

A convenient number for description is 10 such principles, the pillars of Zen.

"Life questions" from common sense may be answered by applying the 10 principles. These questions have been categorised in 51 themes which are subsequently grouped in 4 "Levels", corresponding to the degree of consciousness development they represent.

Any particular person will of course have his or her own questions/problems reflecting a particular background, current situation, etc. If any particular question is sufficiently specific and understood, it should be possible to find a proper location among the levels and themes, thus corresponding to a certain "type" of question. Such types of questions have been used to construct the "Zen Quiz", consisting of typical statements representative for each of the 4 levels of consciousness. Each one of us may be at several different levels in different themes (life situations) but the total score reflects our typical way of living. Usually there will be one predominant and stable level which the individual recognises as the most valid representation of his or her world.

PARADOXICAL "DEVELOPMENT"

The paradox consists in the development as a return to the "primitive", basic innocent mind, a development in reverse, almost a kind of regression. On the other hand, it is a progression in the sense of increased awareness of the Misunderstandings and the appreciation of spontaneity with less need for anxious control.

The progression is characterised by a gradual change from the most physical, material behaviour of conflict (density) to the light, spiritual, non-violent sharing of awareness (space). From perception of good, bad and evil, to "that which just is". From control to acceptance, from acceptance to "make thy will", willingly, to will what happens (but not in a passive, defensive or resigned way).

The second last phase is an ego which wants peace, happiness, harmony (= self development).

The last phase is characterised by an ego which seeks to get rid of the ego (= seeking).

NB! All the stages are still Misunderstandings to some degree. The final stage is really when all the stages are left behind!

How does the whole spectrum look like, all the stages?

1. Firstly, natural innocence is lost. Cunning and competition has taken over.

   Adam has eaten the forbidden fruit of knowledge, Paradise is lost. We are lost in concepts and precepts.

   The dangerous, evil, is out there in the physical world, with alien people. Much like   paranoia, not as a "sickness" but as a "normal" way of perceiving and living. Me as an ego, must protect myself, possibly fight against the external threats in the world. The result is being suspicious, aggressive, violent, perceiving polarity, being obsessed by right and wrong, seeing the world as black and white.

2. Recognising that the good and evil also exist within oneself. When we are not integrated we have an inner conflict going on and are concerned about conscience and morality.

3. Recognising that the inner conflict is artificial or false. Wanting harmony. Striving, confusion, self-contradictions, self-centred, self improvement.

4. Understanding that the ego cannot get rid of the ego. Paradoxes. Hitting the wall. To understand that the problem is fictional. To see that will, ego, me, has to give up, but cannot give up. The ego tries Not doing, but does not succeed because that is also a kind of doing. Experiencing that one actually wants to have the problems. No Resistance. No Investment (of self interest). The death of the Self. Just consciousness. Trading the Personality with the World and Happening. "Own" actions just happen, in the same way as any other kind of events. Returning to the Garden of Eden.

In all seeking, the questions themselves are the very symptoms of the problem. They are therefore also the key to the "Answers", which are not really answers, but understanding that the questions actually are artificial, misunderstandings, self-construed problems, self-misleading, and self-deception!

The help then consists in guiding the attention back to the one who asks. What resides in the questions, what is the motive, why is the person asking? The motive or agenda is usually different from what the person herself or himself believes, sometimes quite the opposite (as when one is projecting one's own worries or weaknesses onto others). This is probably why Dialogue is so essential for many gurus, advisers and therapists. (Combined with the basic condition that there is not much to say *before* someone raises the questions and thereby introduces the problems!). I am tempted also to add that these dialogues, when presented afterwards in book after book, are often rather boring to read. This is just because they are not My problems and therefore not particularly interesting issues for any one apart from the one who is asking. Speaking of gurus, when you understand and appreciate the principle of "Who is asking?", you are in the position of being your own guru. It is up to you.

It is a great opportunity, it is THE opportunity. But it may take some time (= *your* time) before you appreciate it and see what it means.

INDIVIDUAL DEVELOPMENT,
SOLUTION AND CHALLENGES

For every individual the development of self awareness after childhood follows this path:

1. Quite a lot of Misunderstandings, explicitly incorrect theory, rigid belief systems or politics, "knowledge" – with associated actions (behaviour). There is usually a pre-occupation with right and wrong, for us and for our fellow men. This is the first stage in the adult world, after the natural spontaneity and unpredjudiced attitudes of childhood are left behind. Please note that this stage is commonly perceived as a *cultural* characteristic, not as a psychological-individual level of consciousness. The community at this stage of course regards moral pre-occupation as a virtue and as a condition for a civilised society. At the earlier periods of this stage, the polarisation between good and evil is very strong and the sanctions for perceived deviations very extreme. The result is antagonism within own unit as well as towards other groups/societies/belief systems. Gradually,– and historically – and we know this may take a very long time – the antagonism subsides, the external moral becomes more internalised and there is less need to control "the others" as we grow to identify with them. [36,37,62,64]

2. Reflecting, doubt, self development, seeking, self improvement.

3. Insight that also stage 2 is a blind alley. Then one may forthwith discover misconceptions and experience good

situations and better ways of being. Such examples may act as "pointers". From there, there are two ways to go:

a) Gradual un-conditioning, de-conditioning, "neti-neti" (not this, not that). Gradually less pretension, more relaxed attitude, more acceptance towards oneself and others.

b) Sudden insight, "awakening" (as reported in Zen stories and biographies). [6,18,42,43,64,107]

In both cases our attention is turned back to the subject. From Thoughts to Senses. From Virtuality to Reality. From the Apparent to the Actual. Back to the one who is asking.

On this road there are a lot of relationships and situations which are relatively simple to understand, see or experience. But there are also many others which are difficult, or less obvious to get at. Herein resides the Challenge but also the Potential for radical change. Which challenges are we talking about?

Ego, Free Will, me as a Person, me as a Doer, me as apart from the Environment, me as different from the Others, me as Will different from what is Happening, me as Responsible, others as Responsible, Thinking as different from thoughts, Planning and Intention as different from Spontaneity in actions and experience. A recurring Zen theme is the requirement of willingness to die, as a Person, as Ego, letting go of the self identity.

These are the most central, honoured, holy, human, respected, values we possess and cherish. But they are illusions. And it is the misguided one himself or herself who is supposed to find the way out. And who cannot possibly succeed. Just because nothing can be Done. And because the one who is about to do it, does not exist (!). There is nobody around. Luckily there is no need to do anything, because there never was any Problem, anything Wrong from the very beginning. The whole problem, all the stress and striving, all the worrying, have been an Illusion, a Nightmare, a bad dream. When one wakes up, everything is as before and has been all the time, and moreover, everything is OK.

What about the Situation afterwards?

Some teachers say that the less one try to strive for achievement, for desire, or thinking about it, the better. Others say that it is the very strong and genuine wanting that is the condition for liberation. There is probably no single prescription that works for everybody. According to Zen, nothing "works" except as a way of demonstrating the futility, the blind alley. In this context the longest way around, or the most ardent struggle, may thus sometimes turn out as the quickest way to realisation.

Here is a hint to your ego: "Stop Pretending; do you really Want to be free?" "That which you are seeking, is causing you to seek". [62,64,70]

A rule of thumb is that the most obscure or hidden challenges are those which are usually taken as granted or obvious truths in our common sense. The bad news is that there is very little we can do about our frustrations. The good news is that we don't need to do anything. When this is genuinely (experientially, not only theoretically) understood – and that is what Zen or Zen psychology is about – the transformation has thereby already taken place.

WHAT IS THE CRUCIAL ISSUE?

To what degree is it a question about Misunderstanding (and Ignorance), versus Will?

In the first case, the most proper remedies would be education, understanding, and dialogue. In the second case, the remedies should be honesty, observation, discovery, self awareness, self knowing, openness, willingness to spontaneity.

If "the mistake" (!?) is willed, then it brings both good and bad news. Bad: your responsibility. Good: possible to correct, because you can fix it yourself.

Golas [44] says: "No Resistance". With the implication that one is able (willing) to stop doing resistance. That is an exciting possibility! On the other hand, Watts, Arjuna and Harding talk about Grace, implying that there is nothing one can do or not do to attain or receive liberation. [6,54,154]

Identifying the actual cause and best remedy may also be a question of how far one has progresssed in development and awareness. At an early stage, education and questioning about misunderstandings, theories and concepts is probably more than adequate. Later, observation, insight and will (intention) may be more appropriate. To will a mistake, to will the feeling of not having control, to will the feeling of not being present, to will the shortcomings, is an exciting perspective, discovery and possibility. Likewise that the "mistake" is not really a failure, it only appears to be so. "Conditioning" is of course a challenge for rapid change since this kind of learning and de-learning usually works through many repetitions over long periods of time. Krishnamurti [85] promotes sudden and total change, while some others describe gradual de-conditioning of old habits over a long period of time. [62,64] That Seeking, the deliberate need for improvement or enlightenment as such is a problem by itself, a paradoxical challenge. In old times, the Zen masters used this very obstacle as perhaps the main way to liberation, by enhancing the effort and frustration posed by the paradox (expressed as a koan) in order to provoke a letting go of the mind and return to spontaneity (as the natural state of mind).

Which is the most common Misunderstanding?

Perhaps it is this:

Believing in free will (an active Person, Ego, Acting upon an Environment apart from ourselves). This belief permeates both our perception of the healthy person as well as of the neurotic behaviour. Typically we are extremely egocentric when observing other people: we use our own degree of liberation (and energy) as a reference and judge other people's responsibility as if they were like us. These judgements are often surprisingly firm, for instance whether weaknesses like alcoholism, drugs, under-achievement are due to sickness or lack of will.

Friends and family say"pull yourself together", get therapy, be comforted, and then pull yourself together. Self instruction is to improve oneself and others. Blame oneself or others. Vicious circles of responsibility, guilt, control, improvement, ego, ethical conflicts, right and wrong.

In addition, there is the idea that everything can be understood, explained, verbalised, made conscious. That consciousness is an add-on to nature. Admonish our individualism and responsibility and thereby accentuating the person/world division.

Another myth is being tempted to believe that enlightenment is will-based, that it can be attained by will force, by wanting, intentionally. The men and women of wisdom warn us explicitly against that belief which may be rooted in greed, dualism or wishful thinking. Mind cannot get rid of mind, ego cannot eliminate ego. The effort is self defeating and only results in the strengthening of the ego. Only two options remain then:

1. To understand (thoroughly) that there is nothing we can do to attain it.

2. To will what one is, including being insecure, seeking, antagonistic (acceptingly observe our selves, but without adopting laissez-faire as an attitude).

THE SHORTCOMINGS OF COMMON SENSE

It is obvious that one does not want to be in negative states such as anger, aggression, fear, worry and the like. The negative feelings are natural and actually wanted in the sense that you see them as appropriate in their (= your) context. What you do not want is the discomfort or other negative consequences of having such feelings. But you cannot eat your cake and have it too. You must first acknowledge your feelings and your responsibility or participation in creating them. In short, owning them, accepting them as your own doing. The moment you recognise them as your own doing, you are all of a sudden free to neutralise them. How? By simply stopping having them. The challenge was just to recognize that one wants to be in the state in which one is.

In our common sense we do not want these states and we may try/manage to do something about them. Or try to suppress the negative feelings, resulting only in aggravating them or in self-denial and contraction from reality.

This is quite a serious shortcoming of common sense. One cheats oneself thoroughly. Firstly, by pretending to be unintentionally unhappy, then by blaming oneself for being unhappy! When one has made oneself unhappy, then it is paradoxical and almost pathetic to complain about the situation. Likewise, striving to eliminate it. But such an agitation/"improvement" is nevertheless a very clever disguise in order to sustain the misery. Because it is doomed to fail, we run from responsibility while we simultaneously appear to take on responsibility for doing something about it! Or we escape into the role of the victim, declare helplessness and ask for help. While we are glad to reveal the games we play with ourselves, we are left to laugh at our folly. These kinds of happenings are well known in Zen literature. [61,69,126,132,140]

In our dislike of a negative state, there is obvious dualism: **between "I" and "me"**. In the disclaiming of responsibility there is also a powerlessness. If we on the other hand see/ experience/recognize that the condition is willed, there resides a "responsibility", a willed action. And then it is just a matter of stopping to do it! If one really wants to end it, that is. It may well be that the reward of continuing is bigger. But then it is probably of a more dubious character, for example that you shall look helpless, that others shall take care of you, and the like.

We are very clever at these silly games and they are firmly rooted in our culture. Although such myths in principle may be exposed by any individual at any time, it is likely that many laymen as well as professionals (such as therapists) will fiercely defend the myths and sustain them. A lot of pride, pity and pretension are being invested. There is probably no other way of revealing the myths than appealing to self observation. Alternatively, we just wait for our collective common sense to mature. When discomfort in society increases, consciousness sharpens and we get more interested in change.

We may sometimes experience that minor depressions disappear like "dew in the sunshine", when we discover that they were willed. Likewise with some worries. To will, or dare, to allow oneself, to be unconcerned, is what counts. We worry about things, to be on the safe side and avoid being disappointed later on. Trying to escape. But it is the very flight (or wanting to flee) which is the problem.

NB! After having attained stage 4 we are able to consciously, deliberately, facilitate our development. This enhances the process substantially and may result in total liberation.

"The way is through the open door, why is it that so few go through?" [90]

THE WAY OUT IS THROUGH THE OPEN DOOR

The problem is that one believes life is a problem to be solved rather than a mystery to be lived. [125,140,144]

A problem to be understood and solved, in the hope of regaining the happiness we think we had as children.

1. A first step in the right direction is to get some, or a lot of, *experience* with the sad fact that personal problem solving does not work.

2. Then a certain awareness of, or suspicion of, that the attempted problem solving perhaps is a problem in itself, or even the problem itself, and usually creates more problems.

3. Then, to experience that many Problems are due to a Misunderstanding, and thus are illusions or disguise for something else.

4. Then, to **understand** what the Misunderstanding really is about. This understanding is radically opposed to everything we thought was right or important. Indeed it breaks with everything we believed was dearest and holy, personal: identity, independent individual, actions, ego, free will and responsibility. One thing is to hear about this, believe it a little, and increase the understanding. That leads to a need for eliminating the ego. But further understanding reveals that this is not possible. This is primarily because the ego does not really exist, is only an illusion, as it is a misunderstanding in itself.

5. What then? This is the big question. What do you do when you cannot do anything? At the same time, one has at least a theoretical understanding that it is not necessary to do anything. It is not necessary to change/improve, because we all the time we have been in accord with nature (Nature), and cannot deviate even if we wanted to. We believe we

have been, and are, in discord. And we believe and try to do something about it.

6. Then, when one experiences (accepts and feels) that this "wrong" (others faults, our own faults, ego activities, frustration about one's own ego) actually is willed, then the paradoxical happens. The binding ceases to exist and vanishes. Finally one is consciously in accord with Nature, willed (but not "free" will). Experience and actions happen and are accepted, appreciated. Now they are not perceived as wrong or threatening, nor correct and flattering. They are not perceived as a personal achievement or a personal failure. Finally you and the world is one, you are the world and the world is you. And in this world there are other people who you do not any longer perceive as separate from yourself. This sense of belonging, identification – or rather, the sense of identity – provides an immediate and unquestionable acceptance, loving awareness of What Is and, what at the same time, is "you".

The transformation may look like this:

1. Experiencing that personal problem solving does not work.

2. Understanding why, seeing through the illusion.

3. Transcending the apparent conflicts by the awareness of willed frustrations and faults, concurrent with the perception of the unity of the world/me.

Gradually these experiences will turn from being sporadic in the beginning to becoming more frequent and familiar. It is wise to remember that this is not supposed to be hard, strenuous exercise. It is more like play and fun! You shall be less hard on yourself, not more. Otherwise you will not open up and be able to let go of all the defensive games. You cannot be too nice to yourself, nor to others (which are also you, whether you acknowledge it or not).

If there is a Devil, it will be in the escapism, the denied feelings, the frightening aspects, the challenging, the apparently spooky, apparently mean, the wrong, the *un-acceptable*, the *not-understood*, the *unconscious*, the repressed. In short: the not-Me. Embrace also the not-Me. It is only you in disguise.

The way is through the open door.

CHAPTER 9

EPILOGUE

THE NEXT EVOLUTION IN MAN?

Indications of why conscious awareness is the next evolutionary stage in the development of the human mind

1. It addresses all people and thereby concerns human nature.

2. It is not simply learning or culture, but maturation usually over a very long period of time.

3. The development progresses from earlier stages.

4. There is a uniform sequence for all mankind.

5. The process is stable and irreversible. Once the insight has been attained it is not lost or forgotten.

6. Although this evolution is not dependant on biological/ physical maturation, it is a radical mental transformation.

7. It concerns our relationship with nature in a fundamental way, in particular ourselves and our social environment.

8. Any state is qualitatively different from the previous stages.

9. As conflict resolution it has radical consequences for the survival (and well-being) of the species.

10.These criteria have many similarities with the traditional biological criteria for evolution. [25,34,37,38,99,136,155,158]

11.Likewise, the development of consciousness as outlined here, has many similarities with the theories of organic intelligence as well as those of artificial intelligence. [11,12,17,34,37,52,89,92,100,155,160]

EVOLUTION OR JUST A RETURN TO SANITY?

Zen is very clear on appreciating the simple mind, the ordinary mind, returning to a spontaneity resembling the innocent spontaneous state of childhood. It is almost anti-intellectual, or rather anti-academic, pointing to the superficiality of verbalisation, concepts, prescriptions, theories and belief systems. In keeping with this is the focus on the here and now, immediate perceptions, sensations, physical and social reality. That which *is*, rather than what we interpret or believe or want things to be like. Notably, Zen warns against the blind alley and pride of spiritual development and higher mental states. It is not a development, it is rather a return to, or awakening to the original, simple, non-artificial mind. Even more so, because it is not even a return but a discovering of the natural mind which you never left and cannot leave, only pretend to have forgotten. You never left Home. Hence, there is no real development, no higher states. Spiritual pride is moreover one of the great pitfalls of seeking. However, this may not be the whole picture and it is here the psychology may have a say. So there is no advanced state, just the natural, everyday, common mind. On the other hand, Zen is also somewhat paradoxical in this matter, because quite a lot is said about enlightenment, liberation, sudden realization, enlightened people, gurus, etc. Sometimes this realization comes at the same time as a personal experience of a dramatic, profound experience and change of life. The big dichotomy and discrimination is between those who have understood and those who have not. Or between those who know they are liberated and those who don't know (or still believe) they are not liberated. This is indeed a peculiar and interesting perspective and strikes at the very heart of Zen. From a psychological point of view we would say that this difference is nevertheless genuine and profound. Firstly because the insight usually (although not necessarily) requires a large number of experiences and several stages of conscious development. Secondly because the consequences of seeing versus not-seeing, make all the difference in the world. In Zen, there is no real difference between the enlightened and the unenlightened. Technically speaking, this is right. But only if we disregard the preceding conditions of long maturation and likewise the consequences when insight has been attained. The fruits of insight may not necessarily manifest new talents or a change of life situation. [11,71,98,102,110,115] The revolution is on the internal arena, *how* things are done, more than *what* is done.

This *way* of doing things is of no small difference to the person herself or himself, nor to those around them. However, the *transition* from not-knowing to knowing, from confused and frustrated to liberated, is usually no easy endeavour and takes a very, very long time. Unless you are advised and take the hint. Again Zen is right that the liberation *may* happen instantly, for any person at any time. But this has happened very rarely – up to now. It is not possible to achieve deliberately, by intention. The Zen traditions are very much aware of the rareness of enlightenment and the maturity and patience required. The old masters were extremely selective before accepting someone as a student. The patience prescribed, for example, practising full time in monasteries for tens of years, is far beyond what is acceptable in our Western culture. Moreover, a lot of scriptures indicate, in mythical and cosmological terms, a development of consciousness over hundreds of thousands of years. Fortunately, when we look at our own culture today and recent history, it is easy to observe instances from all the different levels of consciousness. Something is happening. Many people are becoming aware of our interconnectedness with the physical environment as well as with other people globally. Along with the challenges the quest for answers is increasing.

The psychological interpretation of Zen, or supplement to Zen, is surely by itself a certain phase in the development of consciousness. The question is – what's next?

REFERENCES

1. Adam, M. (1980). *Womankind.* London: Wildwood House.

2. Adamson, B. (2004). *Presence-Awareness.* Salisbury, UK: Non-duality Press.

3. Adyashanti. (2000). *The Impact of Awakening.* Los Gatos, CA: Open Gate Sangha.

4. Anderson, H, et al. (2008). *The Appreciative Organization.* Chagrin Falls, Ohio:Taos Institute Publications.

5. Arjuna, N.A. (1999). *Relaxing into Clear Seeing.* Grass Valley, CA: SelfXPress.

6. Arjuna, N.A. (2000). *How About Now?* Grass Valley, CA: SelfXPress.

7. Austin, J.H. (1998). *ZEN and the brain.* Cambridge: The MIT Press.

8. Balsekar, R.S. (1992). *Consciousness speaks.* California: Avaita Press.

9. Balsekar, R.S. (1999). *Who Cares?* California: Avaita Press.

10. Bancroft, A. (1979). *Zen.* London: Thames and Hudson.

11. Barron, F. (1969). *Creative Person and Creative Process.* Berkeley, CA: Holt, Rinehart and Winston, Inc.

175

12. Barrow, J.D. (1991). *Theories of Everything*. Oxford: Clarendon Press.

13. Benares, C. (1993). *Zen Without Zen Masters*. Phoenix: New Falcon Publications.

14. Benoit, H. (1974). *The Supreme Doctrine. Psychological Studies in Zen Thought*. New York: The Viking Press.

15. Berge, T. (2007). (In Norwegian): *Oppmerksomt nærvær: En fellesfaktor i psykologisk behandling*. Norsk Psykologisk Tidsskrift, 44, 858-859.

16. Bermudez, J.L. (Ed.) (2006). *Philosophy of Psychology*. New York: Routledge.

17. Bickhard, M.H. & Terveen, L. (1996). *Foundational Issues in Artificial Intelligence and Cognitive Science*. Amsterdam: Elsevier.

18. Blyth, R.H. (1976). *Games Zen Masters Play*. London, New York, Scarborough: New American Library.

19. Boldt, L.G. (1993). *Zen and the Art Making a Living*. New York: Arkana, The Penguin Group.

20. Boldt, L.G. (1997). *Zen Soup*. New York: Arkana, Penguin Books.

21. Bradbury, R. (1996). *Zen in the Art of Writing*. Santa Barbara: Joshua Odell Editions.

22. Brazier, D. (1995). *ZEN therapy*. New York: John Wiley & Sons, Inc.

23. Broughton, J. (1971). *A Long Undressing. Collected Poems*. New York: The Jargon Society.

24. Cain, S. (2013). *Quiet*. London. Penguin Books.

25. Cairns-Smith, A.G. (1985). *Seven Clues to the Origin of Life*. New York: Cambridge University Press.

26. Carse, D. (2006). *Perfect brilliant stillness*. Salisbury, UK: Non-duality Press.

27. Chödrön, P. (2001). *The Places That Scare You*. Boston: Shambhala.

28. Chödrön, P. (2001). *The Wisdom of No Escape*. Boston: Shambhala.

29. Cleary,T. (1994). *Zen Antics*. 100 Stories of Enlightenment. Boston: Shambhala.

30. Dass, R. (1974). *The Only Dance There Is*. New York: Anchor Press.

31. Dass, R. (1985). *Journey of Awakening: a Meditator's Guidebook*. Toronto: Bantam Books.

32. De Mello, A. (1998). *Walking on Water*. New YorK. The Crossroad Publishing Company.

33. Dhiravamsa, V.R. (1984). *The Way of Non-Attachment*. Wellingborough: Turnstone Press.

34. Dreyfus, H.L. & Dreyfus, S.E. (1989). *Mind over Machine*. New York: The Free Press.

35. Duncan, S. (2003). *Present Moment Awareness*. Novato, CA: New World Library.

36. Durkheim, K.G. (1982). *Zen and Us*. New York: E.P. Dutton.

37. Dyson, G.B. (1997). *Darwin among the Machines. The evolution of global intelligence*. Cambridge, Massachusetts: Perseus Books.

38. Feldman, C.R. & Kuyken, W. (2019). *Mindfulness. Ancient Wisdom Meets Modern Psychology*. New York, NY. The Guilford Press.

39. Ferguson, D. (2001). *No Carrot. Just the zen of it*. Devon: The Foundation.

40. Foster, J. (2008). *Life without a centre*. Salisbury, UK: Non-duality Press.

41. Gaarder, A.P. (2019). *May Psychology be an Empirical Science?* (in Norwegian). Norway. Høgskolen i Innlandet.

42. Gibbs, J.J. (1990). *Dancing with Your Books: the Zen Way of Studying.* New York: Penguin Books.

43. Gill, N. (2004). *Already Awake.* Salisbury, UK: Non-duality Press.

44. Golas, T. (1981). *The Lazy Man's Guide to Enlightenment.* Toronto: Bantam Books.

45. Goswani, A. (1995). *The Self-Aware Universe.* New York: Penguin Putnam Inc.

46. Guenther, H.V. & Trungpa. C. (1975). *The Dawn of Tantra.* Boulder & London: Shambala

47. Hanh, T.N. (1976). *The Miracle of Being Awake.* Kandy, Sri Lanka: Buddhist Publication Society.

48. Hanh, T.N. (1987). *The Miracle of Mindfulness.*Boston: Beacon press.

49. Hanh, T.N. (2001). *Anger.* New York: Riverhead Books.

50. Hanh, T.N. (2002). *No Death, No Fear.* New York: Penguin Putnam, Inc.

51. Harari. Y.N. (2016). *Sapiens.* Oslo: Bazar.

52. Harari. Y.N. (2016). *Homo Deus.* London: Harvill Secker.

53. Harding, D. E. (1979). *The Hierarcy of Heaven & Earth.* Gainesville: University Presses of Florida.

54. Harding, D.E. (1986). *On Having No Head.* London: Penguin Books.

55. Harding, D. E. (1988). *The Little Book of Life and Death.* New York: Arkana, Routledge.

56. Harding, D.E. (1990). *Head off stress.* London: Penguin Books.

57. Harding, D. E. (1997). *The Science of the 1ˢᵗ Person.* London: The Shollond Trust.

58. Harding, D. E. (1998). *Look for Yourself.* Encinitas, CA: Inner Directions Publishing.

59. Harding, D. E. (2000). *Face to No-Face.* Encinitas, CA: Inner Directions Publishing.

60. Harding, D. E. (2002). *To Be and not to be, that is the answer.* London: Watkins Publishing.

61. Harris, S. (2012). *Free Will.* New York, NY. Free Press.

62. Harris. S. (2012). *The Moral Landscape.* UK: Black Swan

63. Harris, S. (2013). *Lying.* U.S. Four Elephants Press.

64. Harris. S. (2015). *Waking Up.* UK: Penguin Random House.

65. Harrison, S. (2002). *Doing Nothing.* New York: Penguin Putnam, Inc.

66. Herrigel, E. (1969). *The Method of Zen.* London: Routledge and Kegan Paul.

67. Hillig, C. (2001). *The Way IT is.* Ojai, CA: Black Dot Publications.

68. Hofstadter, D.R. & Dennett, D.C. (1982). *The Mind's I.* New York: Bantam Books.

69. Huber, C. (1984). *The Key and the Name of the Key is Willingness.* Murphys, CA: A Center for the Practise of Zen Buddhist Meditation.

70. Huber, C. (1990). *That Which You Are Seeking is Causing You to Seek.* Murphys, CA: A Center for the Practise of Zen Buddhist Meditation.

71. Huber, C. (1995). *Nothing Happens Next.* Murphy's, CA: Keep It Simple Books.

72. Huber, C. (1995). *The Fear Book*. Mountain View, CA: Zen Center.

73. Huber, C. (1996). *Being Present in the Darkness*. New York: The Berkely Publishing Group.

74. Huber, C. (2001). *There is Nothing Wrong with You for TEENS*. Murphy's, CA: Keep It Simple Books.

75. Humphreys, C. (1985). *ZEN a Way of Life*. London: Teach Yourself Books.

76. Hunter, D.; Bailey, A.; Taylor, B. (1992). *The Zen of Groups. A Handbook for People Meeting with a Purpose*. Cambridge, Great Britain: Gower Publishing.

77. Kane, A & Kane, S. (1999). *Working on yourself doesn't work*. New York: ASK Productions, Inc.

78. Katagiri, D. (1988). *Returning to Silence*. Boston: Shambala.

79. Katie, B. (2002). *Loving What Is*. New York: Harmony Books.

80. Katie, B. (2005). *I Need Your Love- Is That True?* New York: Harmony Books.

81. Kersschot, J. (2004). *This Is It*. London: Watkins Publishing.

82. Khyentse, D. (1993). *Enlightened Courage*. New York: Snow Lion Publications.

83. Klein, J. (1978). *Be Who You Are*. London & Dulverton: Watkins.

84. Klein, J. (1986). *The Ease of Being*. Durham, Nort Carolina: The Acorn Press.

85. Krishnamurti, J. (1996). *Total Freedom*. SanFrancisco: HarperSanFrancisco.

86. Krishnamurti, J. (1972). *You are the World*. London: Krishnamurti Foundation.

87. Krishnamurti, J. (2000). *To Be Human.* Boston: Shambhala.

88. Kurzweil, R. (1999). *The Age of the Spiritual Machines.* New York: Penguin Books.

89. Kwee, G.T.; Gergen, K.J.; Fusako, K. (2006). *Horizons in Buddhist Psychology.* Ohio. The Taos Institute Publication.

90. Laing, R.D. (1960) *The Divided Self: An Existential Study in Sanity and Madness.* Harmondsworth: Penguin.

91. Leach, E. (1969). *A Runaway World?* London: Oxford University Press.

92. Leary, T. (2001). *Your Brain Is God.* Oakland, Publishers Group West.

93. Levine, S. & O. (1989). *Who Dies?* New York: Random House, Inc.

94. Low, A. (1993). *The butterfly's dream. In search of the roots of Zen.* Boston: Charles E. Tuttle   Company, Inc.

95. Marcel, A.J. & Bisiach, E. (eds.). (1992). *Consciousness in Contemporary Science.* Oxford: Clarendon Press.

96. McMullan, J. & Levin, M. (1996). *Instant Zen.* Rutland, Vermont: C.E.Tuttle Company.

97. Menezes, R. (2005). *Blood Washing Blood. A Zen Perspective of Psychotherapy.* London: Janus Publishing Company.

98. Moore, T. (2001). *Original Self. Living with Paradox and Autenticity.* New York: Harper Collins.

99. Moravec, H. (1998). *Mind Children: the Future of Robot and Human Intelligence.* Cambridge, Massachusetts: Harvard University Press.

100. Moravec, H. (1999). *Robot: mere Machine to Transcendent Mind.* Oxford: Oxford University Press.

101. Morrison, S. (2000). *Open and Innocent*. New York: Twenty First Century Renaissance.

102. Müller, A. (2019). *You Will Never Be Free*. UK. Milton Keynes. Books on Demand, Norderstedt.

103. Nadeen, S. (2000). *From Seekers to Finders*. Carlsbad, CA: Hay House, Inc.

104. Osho. (1991). *The New Child*. Amsterdam: Osho Publikaties

105. Osho. (2001). *The Book of Wisdom*. Pune, India: The Rebel Publishing House.

106. Osho. (2001). *Zen: The Path of Paradox*. New York: St. Martin's Griffin.

107. Parson, T. (2004). *Invitation to Awaken*. Carlsbad, CA: Inner Directions Publishing.

108. Pinker. S. (2018). *Enlightenment Now*. UK. Penguin Random House.

109. Regardie, I. (1985). *The Lazy Man's Guide to Relaxation*. Phoenix, Arizona: Falcon Press.

110. Renz, K. (2005). *The Myth of Enlightenment*. Carlsbad: Inner Directions.

111. Rodegat, P & Stanton, J. (eds.) (1989). *Emmanuel's Book II. The Choice for Love*. New York, Toronto. London, Sydney, Auckland: Bantam Books.

112. Rychlak, J.F. (1997). *In Defense of Human Consciousness*. Washington: The American Psychological Association.

113. Sampson, E.E. (2008). *Celebrating the Other*. Chagrin Falls, Ohio:Taos Institute Publications.

114. Salzberg, S. (1997). *A Heart as wide as the World*. Boston: Shambhala.

115. Salzman, B.W. (2004). *Being a Buddha on Broadway*. Carlsbad: Inner Directions Publishing.

116. Sayadaw, M. (1976) *Practical Insight Meditation.* Peradeniya, Sri Lanka: Supra Printers.

117. Schiller, D. (1994). *The little Zen Companion.* New York: Workman Publishing.

118. Searle, J. (1989). *Minds, Brains & Science.* London: Penguin Books.

119. Simler. K. & Hanson. R. (2018). *The Elephant in the Brain.* New York: Oxford University Press.

120. Smedslund, J. (1997). *The Structure of Psychological Common Sense.* London: Lawrence Erlbaum Associates, Publishers

121. Smedslund, J. (2004). *Dialogues About A New Psychology.* Chagrin Falls, Ohio:Taos Institute Publications.

122. Smedslund, J. (2016). *Why Psychology Cannot be an Empirical Science.* Integrative Psychological and Behavioral Science

123. Sluyter, D. (2001). *The Zen Commandments.* New York: Penguin Books.

124. Stuart, D. (1983). *Alan Watts.* New York: Scarborough Books.

125. Sudo, P.T. (2000). *Zen Sex.* New York: HarperCollins Publishers Inc.

126. Swami, S.P. (transl). (1978). *The Bhagavad Gita.* London: Faber and Faber.

127. Tagore, R. (1963). *The Religion of Man.* London: Unwin Books.

128. Tolle, E. (2003). *Stillness Speaks.* Novato/Vancouver: New World Library/Namaste Publishing.

129. Trungpa. C. (1969). *Meditation in Action.* Boulder: Shambala

130. Trungpa. C. (1973). *Cutting through Spiritual Materialism*. Berkeley, CA: Shambala.

131. Trungpa. C. (ed). (1976). *Garuda IV. The Foundations of Mindfulness*. Berkeley & London: Shambala.

132. Tsu, L. (1972). *Tao Te Ching*. New York: Vintage Books. Random House.

133. Tulku, S. & Berzin, A. (eds.). (1980). *A Compendium of Ways of Knowing*. New Delhi: Library of Tibetan Works and Archives

134. Vienne, V. (1998). *The Art of Doing Nothing*. New York: Clarkson Potter Publishers.

135. Vollestad, J. (2007). (In Norwegian): *Oppmerksomt nærvær: Meditative teknikker som utgangspunkt for psykologisk behandling*. Norsk Psykologisk Tidsskrift, 44, 860-867.

136. Watts, A. (1970). *Nature, Man and Woman*. New York: Random House.

137. Watts, A. (1972). *The Art of Contemplation*. New York: Pantheon Books, Random House.

138. Watts, A. (1972). *The Spirit of Zen*. London: John Murray

139. Watts, A. (1973). *Beyond Theology*. New York: Vintage Books. Random House.

140. Watts, A. (1973). *The Book on the taboo against knowing who you are*. England: Abacus.

141. Watts, A. (1973). *The Supreme Identity*. London: Wildwood House.

142. Watts, A. (1973). *This is It*. New York: Pantheon Books, Random House.

143. Watts, A. (1974). *Cloudhidden, Whereabouts Unknown*. London: Lowe and Brydone.

144. Watts, A. (1975). *Psychotherapy East and West*. New York: Vintage Books, Random House.

145. Watts, A. (1975). *The Two Hands of God*. New York: Collier Books.

146. Watts, A. (1976). *Zen Edge*. London: Thames and Hudson

147. Watts, A. (1977). *The Essential Alan Watts*. Berkeley, Ca: Celestial Arts.

148. Watts, A. (1979). *Tao*. Middlesex, England: Penguin Books.

149. Watts, A. (1980). *Om. Creative Meditations*. Berkeley, CA: Celestial Arts.

150. Watts, A. (1997). *Taoism: Way Beyond Seeking*. Boston: Tuttle Publishing.

151. Watts, A. (1997). *Zen and the Beat Way*. Boston: Tuttle Publishing.

152. Watts, A. (2000). *Still the Mind*. Novato, CA: New World Library.

153. Watts, A. (2000). *What is Zen?* Novato: New World Library

154. Watts, A. (2003). *Become What You Are*. Boston: Shambhala

155. Watts, A. (2020). Just So. Canada. Boulder CO.

156. Watts, D. (1986). *Zen Sensualism*. Oakland, CA: Hart-Eden Press.

157. Wheeler, J. (2006). *Right here, Right now*. Salisbury, UK: Non-duality Press.

158. Wilber, K. (1996). *A Brief History of Everything*. Boston & London: Shambala.

159. Wing, R.L. (1986). *The Tao of Power*. Wellingborough: The Aquarian Press.

160. Wolfram, S. (2002). *A New Kind of Science*. Champaign, IL: Wolfram Media, Inc.

Author & son

ABOUT THE AUTHOR

Stein Gaarder (mag.art.) is currently working as a court expert for children and family affairs. He spends much of his time at the cabin by a lake in the South of Norway.

Being an accredited specialist in organisational psychology the author has nevertheless been a student and practitioner of Zen for more than 40 years.

He has conducted psychological research and training at the University of Oslo and in the private industry for three decades. A major part of his professional career has been devoted to human factors and reducing accidents in extreme work environments within the shipping, offshore and space industries. He was a NATO advisor in the follow-up of the Challenger Space Craft Accident.

His engagement span from being a co-author of the book "Children, Environment and Development", coordinator for refugees & immigrants in Norway and research on "Human Reliability in Manned Space Missions" (The European Space Agency).

In 1997 he was invited to apply as chief of the division of Research & Organisational Development of the United Nations, New York.

E-mail: stein.gaarder@vikenfiber.no

Printed in Great Britain
by Amazon

19804521R00119